Teaching Literacy

Also available from Continuum:

Martin Blocksidge (ed.) *Teaching Literature 11–18*

Andy Goodwyn *English in the Digital Age*

Manjula Datta (ed.) *Bilinguality and Literacy*

Morag Styles, Gabrielle Cliff Hodges and Mary Jane Drummond (eds) *Tales, Tellers and Texts*

Bernice E. Cullinan and Diane G. Person (eds) *Encyclopedia of Children's Literature*

Nikki Gamble and Nick Easingwood *ICT and Literacy*

Teaching Literacy

A Creative Approach

Fred Sedgwick

CONTINUUM
London and New York

Continuum
The Tower Building, 11 York Road, London SE1 7NX
370 Lexington Avenue, New York, NY 10017-6503

www.continuumbooks.com

First published 2001

British Library Cataloguing-in-Publication Data
A catalogue record for this book is available from the British Library.

ISBN 0-8264-5171-3 (hardback)
　　　0-8264-5172-1 (paperback)

Typeset by CentraServe Ltd, Saffron Walden, Essex
Printed and bound in Great Britain by Cromwell Press, Trowbridge, Wilts

Contents

Acknowledgements

Many thanks to Anthony Haynes, editor at Continuum, who showed an extraordinary interest in this project from the start, almost as though he didn't have a professional interest in it.

Acknowledgements are due to the following schools, who entertained me, let me work with their children and teachers, paid me, and allowed me to take some of the children's work home.

Ashwell Primary, Herts; Bedford Preparatory; Cliff Lane Primary, Ipswich, Suffolk; Donnington Middle, Oxford; Dundale Primary, Tring, Herts; East Bergholt Primary, Suffolk; Fairfields Primary, Cheshunt, Herts; Fleetville Primary, St Albans, Herts; Great Massingham Primary, Norfolk; Heybridge Primary, Essex (especially, once again, Sophie Chipperfield); Hollesley Primary, Suffolk (thank you, Caroline Moore, for the biographies); Ickleford Primary, Hitchin, Herts (thank you, Elaine Sansom, for the Jabberwocky translation idea); Bealings, Ipswich, Suffolk (especially Duncan 'The Saint' Bathgate, for his children's descriptions of the mean characters based on Uriah Heep); Peartree Spring Junior, Stevenage, Herts; Radburn Primary, Letchworth, Herts; Rosehill Primary, Ipswich, Suffolk; St Ipployt's, Hitchin, Herts; St John's Primary, Ipswich, Suffolk; Tattingstone Primary, Ipswich, Suffolk; Tacolneston Primary, Norfolk; Pinkwell Primary, Hayes, London; Wilson Primary, Reading, Berkshire (thank you, Sally Wilson, for your confession).

Preface

In a recent book, *Shakespeare and the Young Writer* (1999b), I printed the words below. They were written by an 11-year-old girl in a Suffolk school. She was responding to my reading of Mercutio's great Queen Mab speech from *Romeo and Juliet* (1:4:54ff). I read Lizbeth's writing from the pulpit of Ely Cathedral on 23 April 1998, on an occasion when the then Bishop of Ely read from the King James Bible, and Philippa Pearce read from her novel *Tom's Midnight Garden*, and when children from local schools read poems that they had written. This was St George's Day, of course but, more to the point, it was Shakespeare's probable birthday and his anniversary.

O then I see Queen Mab has been with you:
She is the trees' bark shaper, and she comes
In a shape as round as our earth itself,
A small particle of magical fate,
Travelling, floating with the natural breeze.
Through polar bears' hairs she explores the ice.
Her spherical carriage gracefully soars
Looked on by inhabitants, young and old,
Infinite omens and curses are chanted:
The portholes in her sphere of glistening webs,
Her seat inside of shining beetle's shell,
Her silk jacket red as Jupiter's glow,
Her jewels of water shoes of tropical heat,
Her chauffeurs red-jacketed wire-haired dogs,
Abyssinian, native bred, small kings.

Each of my books seem to contain in them the seed of the next one. Seeing at close hand what power children could bring to their writing when taught by William Shakespeare, I decided to see what they could do when faced with other writers teaching them. Hence this new book.

Preliminary note

Most of the chapters in this book are composed of the following elements. Sometimes the elements are mixed up; sometimes they are separated:

- An introduction, with some basic information about the writers in the chapter, or the sources.
- Some autobiographical material. I have included this because, as many conversations during residential courses have taught me, it is enlightening to compare experiences as readers with other enthusiasts.
- Passages of literature.
- Some work of mine inspired by, or derived from, those passages.
- Children's work inspired by, or derived from, those passages, and commentary on what the children have written.
- Commentary on this writing, and on the teaching involved.

Introduction

SCHOOLING AND EDUCATION: OFFICIAL AND UNOFFICIAL

> 'What', it will be questioned, 'when the sun rises, do you not see a round disc of fire somewhat like a guinea?' 'Oh no, no. I see an innumerable company of the heavenly crying: Holy Holy Holy is the Lord God Almighty.' (William Blake, 'A Vision of the Last Judgement', 1810)

I begin with what seems to me to be an undeniable truth. Schooling is mostly official. It always has been. It derives from the views and interests of our masters and mistresses: politicians, inspectors and advisers. These views and interests – corrupt in the sense that they pretend to be about the interests of children and are really about statistics – are filtered through and then further corrupted by elements that have little to do with learning: the media and its need for sales and influence, and the politicians' needs for re-election.

While schooling has always followed tracks laid down by those masters and mistresses, in recent years our elders and betters have built and put in place means of ensuring we follow them. We are ruled by OFSTED (the Office for Standards in Education, the main inspection body in schools, colleges and local educational authorities in the United Kingdom). We are ruled by league tables, Standard Attainment Tests, lists of scores, mean-spirited categories such as 'satisfactory', 'serious weaknesses' and 'special measures'. We are ruled by the need for short-term, long-term and mid-term plans. We are ruled by performance-related pay. Any teacher can continue this list.

There is an especially chilling aspect to this officialdom and its gradually increasing power. As Michael Rosen writes (1994) 'The new educational orthodoxy, as represented in the National Curriculum documents . . . has no time for speculation on childhood.' The child is absent from the documents that drop into schools every day. Officialdom has no time, either, despite its ludicrous requests during OFSTED inspections for more 'awe and wonder', for the spiritual. To use Blake's exclamation, it is all guinea and no holiness. While it recognizes (like Lord Darlington) that we are all 'in the gutter', it has no notion that some of us are 'looking at the stars', that some of us recognize the value of things (Lord Darlington again), and not just their price (Wilde, 1990).

The result has been that schooling has, since the early 1990s, become entirely official and therefore entirely concerned with statistics, not children; entirely concerned with what can be seen and measured, rather than what cannot be seen, but which lives with and through and in our being. There are exceptions, though: rare schools that glow like reflected points of light in a polluted river. In these schools, headteachers and their staff have summoned up all their courage, their intellectual resourcefulness and their heart, and continued to do what they know they should do. These schools, in my experience, are characterized, at the beginnings of OFSTED inspections, by a determination on the part of the headteacher to make clear to him or herself what the school stands for, and then to make that stand clear to advisers and inspectors. They are also characterized, more generally, by honour given to the arts, painting, poetry, music and even (in these dark days) dance and drama. There is work from schools that prepare their moral ground in this courageous way throughout this book.

In most schools, on the other hand, chances for spontaneity are gone. Older teachers remember with sad pleasure days when, for example, an enthusiast for snakes or birds of prey visited the school, and it led to two weeks intensive work in language, art and science; or when an electric storm stimulated poems and paintings, dance and drama, produced under the storm with palpable excitement and fear in the classroom. Such moments are hard to find now when every moment of a classroom's life has to be accounted for on form after form after form; when every school moment has to be measured and assessed.

Most classrooms are now extensions of our bosses' offices. This is a stark truth to teachers who were brought up in teaching to see classrooms as places where communities of scholars worked together, environments where children learned about themselves and the world that they have inherited. Now, the bosses look through the glass doors, the glass windows, to check what we the teachers are doing. They interrupt us while we are doing it. Our headteacher is the front-line inspector. Between OFSTED inspections, the inspection goes on, as local 'advisers' 'monitor' what teachers are doing in response to the last OFSTED inspection, and what they are doing in anticipation of the next. Orwell's Winston Smith would have recognized all this. I exaggerate? During an OFSTED inspection, one lesson was deemed 'unsatisfactory' because the shared reading part of the literacy hour had lasted three minutes longer than prescribed.

Education (this word, by the way, is in OFSTED's name merely in an institutional sense, and is not to be confused with learning) is different. It is almost never official. It barely exists until teachers and children together race *across* the tracks, or go to the *other side* of them; until they begin the discovery of what is unknown, or known and then discarded, by those officials. Until teachers and children subvert what those masters and mistresses require of them, education will not happen: only schooling will. 'It is the business of education' wrote Lawrence Stenhouse in his 1976 book, 'to make us freer and more creative.' It is not the business of education to make us pegs for appropriate holes.

Lady Bracknell famously said in Oscar Wilde's *The Importance of Being Earnest* that 'fortunately, in England, at any rate, education produces no effect whatsoever. If it did, it would prove a serious danger to the upper classes, and probably lead to acts of violence in Grosvenor Square.' The reason for education's impotence is that much of what passes for it – and this is just as true now as it was in Wilde's day – is really schooling. After a moment's thought, it is not difficult to produce a list of activities that children have been given that have no discernible reference to education: singing and acting in *Joseph and his Amazing Technicolor Dreamcoat* (not *again!*); taking a minor part in the same play (or any other play) and therefore hanging about for ages doing nothing while the stars are rehearsed; filling in templated shapes, those shapes having been designed by a teacher with a background (it would seem) in shop-window display; copying out writing for display (not to be confused with redrafting); struggling to remember what a phoneme is; singing 'Little Donkey'; being first reserve all season in a football or netball team; making fair copies (not to be confused with redrafts) of poems and stories ... It is worth noting that many of these pointless activities, while flourishing before the current torrent of officialdom described above, still carry on now unaffected by successive governments' so-called quality control.

Elements of what I will call 'mere schooling' have always been present, *necessarily*, in classrooms. Teachers protect children from themselves, each other and their environment, with rules and dinner registers, with walls and instruction, with sanctions of various kinds. But much of this controlling behaviour is violent, bureaucratic and sometimes simply vindictive. (Overheard in a staffroom at lunchtime: 'Stella's being vile again. Got anything unpleasant for her to do?' 'Get her to copy out two pages of her reading book. She'll hate that).'

Parents (who, after their children, are most concerned with this) may glimpse, fleetingly, among all this administrative and sometimes penal detritus, like a lizard glimpsed among dry greenery on a rock, a flicker of learning. But they should not count on it. There are traces of learning in it all, just as there are traces of jazz on JazzFM. No more. Flickers of learning are now and then present in documents like the following, though management is the main thrust of them: *English: The National Curriculum for England* (Department for Education and Employment (DFEE), and Qualifications and Curriculum Authority (QCA), *Using Information and Communications Technology to Meet Teaching Objectives in English* Teacher Training Agency (TTA), *National Standards for Qualified Teacher Status* (TTA) and *Initial Teacher Training National Curriculum for Primary English*. Aspects of education relevant to the concerns of this book that are mentioned in those documents are signalled in the index.

But, mostly, learning is in the child's eyes as she talks with the teacher who is intent on both the child's learning and his or her own. It is there when a child's mind and heart are active in the search for connections between his or her known world and unknown world (always, at least at first, glimpsed through a glass, darkly). It is there when a child writes, with poise and frankness, about the death of a grandmother:

Fear no more, the knitting's done.
Fear no more, the garden's growing.
Fear no more, the thunder's blown away,
Fear no more, the toad's OK
and is still mucking the leaves.
Fear no more, your son's teddy's safe
and all your possessions are in good hands.

Fear no more the heart attacks and hospitals.
Fear no more, the blackberries are picked
and the jam tarts are done.
Fear no more, Grandad's well,
Fear no more of amusing me.

(Anna, 10)

This child, importantly, is communicating (National Curriculum, English Key Stages 1–4, p. 8) both with herself and her readers and listeners something of her love for, and her reaction to her loss of, her grandmother. But such an official account sells the piece short. She is doing many other things. For an account of the lesson during which Anna wrote this, and what I think she was learning as she wrote, see Sedgwick, 1999b.

And (this is rarely counted important enough) education is present when teachers learn – from the children that they teach, and from each other as they research their teaching together. If teachers ever learn again the importance of this collaborative activity, they will regain some control over their work with children. They will lift themselves, however slowly, however painfully, from the shameful status of hired hands to which they have been relegated by the mechanistic policies of successive governments. They will learn again something of the holiness that is involved in close attention to the child, and something of the squalor that is involved in concentrating on the guinea.

All art is political because when we strive to create something that will, we hope, take on an existence, however frail, outside ourselves – a drawing, a song, a poem, a story, a carving, a dance – we tell managers and other officials something that they need to be told at every moment of their waking lives: that we, the managed, are human beings, not numbers. That our places are amongst other human beings, in kitchens and living rooms, in gardens and parks, in churches and temples, in restaurants and pubs, in studies and studios, not on checklists of test scores. There is, of course, no evidence that managers recognize this need. Politicians and inspectors talk about raising standards and raising test scores as though they are the same thing. They are extreme materialists, and wouldn't understand an achievement that they cannot measure if it exploded in their faces.

A New Form of Officialdom

Walk into almost any primary school today, and you will find *Elmer the Elephant* and other books by David McKee. I know them well, because I used to read them now and then with my son when he was small. I am glad that they have become part of the norm. But I am disturbed that they have become something very like official texts. They have become books that have been chosen by the political and administrative elite. Whoever should choose what young children read in schools (and who should – teachers? parents? the children themselves?), it should not be politicians. Much as a school sponsored by British American Tobacco will be cripplingly biased in its health education, a school where politicians dictate what is read will, sooner or later, be biased one way or another.

For different reasons, the same has happened with paintings. Those presented in reproduction to schools by the Sainsbury's Pictures for School Scheme are excellent, but they have become the only famous pictures that many children see. They have become official. All children now have the opportunity to see *Two Boys and a Girl Making Music* by Jan Molenaer, *The Woodman's Daughter* by John Millais, *Child with Dove* by Picasso and *Orthodox Boys* by Bernard Perlin. Of course, this scheme has greatly enriched the appearance of walls in primary schools. But I have to ask how much the disturbing emergent sexuality of one of the pictures and the fear of racism in another have become articulated in schools. I suspect that the underlying subjects of these pictures have been largely ignored, subjects which are of great interest to all children. The pictures have become disempowered by becoming official. They have become ornaments. And also, how helpful is it to other paintings to be implicitly relegated to the status of unofficial art?

Using Classic Texts to Subvert

For this book I have tried to build on this foundation: that literature in English, other than these new quasi-official texts, could be used to teach children from 8 to 13 years old. This 'other' traditional literature could help them to learn through writing. Conventionally, subversions would have meant using unfashionable modern books, printed by small publishing houses in small editions, perhaps with left-leaning material in them. Chris Searle's excellent 1983 anthology of poetry *Wheel Around the World* comes to mind, and so does Michael Rosen's book about teaching poetry *I See a Voice* (1982) – two books that concentrate on poems about, by, and for the common people, the dispossessed. But instead, I have worked with what are called 'classics of children's literature', and some classics that were never intended for children at all.

Of course, such books had been used by teachers for ages. I have written a book (Sedgwick, 1999b) about using Shakespeare as a teacher, and more work by children following Shakespeare's example appears here. I remembered books I had enjoyed as a child; books that I enjoyed reading with and to my son; books that I had discovered and books that I had never conceived as having anything to say to children. All these books were old books, books that were out of copyright.

Many writers that I would have loved to have used were eliminated by this latter (practical) consideration. Children enjoy Rudyard Kipling's work and not only his *Jungle Book*. Poems like 'Tommy' and 'Danny Deever', harsh, dangerous pieces about the military life (both are easily found in Larkin, 1973), will hold the appalled attention of a top junior class. I have the impression that stories in James Joyce's *Dubliners*, the travel writing of D. H. Lawrence and some of the early poems of Yeats have much to offer schoolchildren, but work on them will wait until I have time, and the writers are out of copyright.

In a pub in Newmarket, Anthony Haynes, my editor, and I reflected on these issues, and slowly this book grew from seed status. How interesting it would be, we thought, to see giants of literature in a subversive role that, presumably, they would never have seen themselves in.

An Autobiographical Thread

I have sewn an autobiographical thread through my book. I have always been obsessed with books, and with reading, and I believe that my account of my relationship with books will (to change my metaphor) strike chords with my readers. I have always envied writers who have had two experiences denied to me. The first is an apparently total recall of significant moments of early childhood. I envy this capacity because, as Wordsworth knew long before Freud made an industry of it, early childhood is the most electrically charged subject for writers. A child solemnly told me (and then wrote it down) that she 'remembered just before I was born. I was in my mummy's tummy. She was watching television. She was watching "The Bill".' [What was it like in your mummy's tummy?] 'It was dark.' My son remembers cutting his finger in France when he was 3. Josie (a teacher on a course) remembers looking out from her pram, through the lacing around the canopy at the clear sky.

I used to be sceptical about stories like this until I heard about Benjamin Britten. He claimed that he remembered his birth, and the 'sound of rushing water'. (Donald Mitchell quoted in Carpenter, 1992). I still think that many early memories are in fact memories of being told about events or, even more frequently, they are memories of photographs, refreshed every time the album is produced on a quiet evening when there is not much on television. For example, when I try to remember, while walking around the streets where I live, my son's early life (he has just gone to university and, missing him, I am much given to walking and thinking about him) I find that the moments from his life that I recall are moments recorded in the photographs that run in a line across the top of the corkboard in my study where I type this. I do not really believe this girl's account about being born – it is a story told to her many times – while I accept that it made a powerful moment in a school, and a powerful piece of writing.

The second experience that I lack is the reading of great books at a very early age. Sometimes I am irritated by, sometimes merely envious of, accounts of the voracious devouring of *Robinson Crusoe* at 6, Graham Greene 'entertainments' at 10, and *Paradise Lost* at 14. Michael Rosen spoke recently on Radio 4 about discovering *Dubliners* and *A Portrait of the Artist as a Young Man* by James Joyce in his teens. My brother (two years my junior) remembers reading *David Copperfield* when he was still at primary school. He also remembers 'waking up early to read Geoffrey Trease novels'. My patchy memory recalls more intermittent, less elevated reading than that: comics, of course; hymns; adventure novels by now forgotten (at least by me) writers; the thrillers of Dornford Yates and 'Sapper', the author of the Bulldog Drummond novels; the Anthony Buckeridge 'Jennings' books; school stories with titles like *The Fifth Form at St Dominic's*. I remember noting at the time that I tended to read school stories that were about boys (no, never girls) who were three or four years older than me.

Looking over a second draft of the above, I note how this bits-and-pieces experience of reading has influenced my writing of this book. It anticipates a post-modernist view of literature, writing and reading, in that nearly all experiences of reading are fragmentary. A child reads advertisements before he or she reads books, and all sorts of non-literary material surrounds me as I sit here writing. I am surrounded by the spines of books. I look up occasionally and read the maker's name on my printer and my computer; the make of the car on the opposite side of the street; my scribbled notes pinned to the corkboard; notes from my son (or even the envelope that contained one, scrawled on which is my favourite word, 'Dad'); a newspaper music review headline containing details of a CD I might buy eventually; captions to postcards; and even an enamel badge celebrating a football victory.

Most reading is like this. My early reading of all sorts of rubbish certainly was. And now, even when it comes to books, I do not read one through, and then find another. I have several on the go: a literary biography that is alternately boring and distressing me, and which I might well have given up if it were not for my puritan spirit (unquenchable, unfortunately); a detective novel; a book of poems by a current poet, Ruth Padel; *The Winter's Tale*; a huge book of literary criticism whose insights I hope to use for my work on this book; *Twelfth Night* (again); *History in English Words* by Owen Barfield. All of these are routinely put by for the morning paper and the post, and for magazines like *The Oldie* and *Private Eye*. I drop any reading to read the football report on my team's game.

But we will start with commonest kind of prose, at least as convention sees it: the story. As I write, I am going to keep in mind Blake's distinction between the guinea and the heavenly host. And if you, as an agnostic or an atheist, are put off by the second half of that distinction, I suggest that the part of you that is sensitive to what materialism, the machine, has done to our society, not least in its schooling, might reflect on what you will put in the place of the holiness and the heavenly host.

1

Fiction

FALSE STORIES

I told my story to them, and I began to understand.
(Emily Roeves)

There are at least three serious problems about the writing of fiction in primary schools. The first is the problem of what I will call the 'false story'. In primary schools, until quite recently, during the teaching and study of any given topic, children have traditionally been told to 'write a story about it'. The subject of the story might be anything: a nature walk, a visit from a musician, a play by another class, a trip to a castle or a cathedral, a coach journey to a museum or to an art gallery. Whatever it is, the children have always known, know, will know, what they have to do: that is, to write words and sentences about whatever their experience is.

But in fact none of the prose examples that resulted from this activity (unless by some quirk) was a story at all. What appeared under the child's hand might, of course, have had a place in a number of other honourable prose genres: it might have been, for example, reportage. It might have been a writing-up of a scientific observation. It might have been a diary or a journal entry. It might have suited repackaging as a letter. It was almost never fiction: it was what I have called a 'false story'.

Second, being *told* to write a story is not the same as being *taught* to write one. I have never seen anything like an attempt by any teacher to help children to learn what fiction is, or how they might achieve an effect: atmosphere, for example, or crisp dialogue, or creating suspense. And I have never made that attempt myself. Children left to themselves always write chronologically, the dull word 'then' symbolizing a strictly linear approach. This approach betrays no sense of what flashbacks can help a writer to achieve, or telling the events of a story in a different order from the one in which they happened, or giving versions of events from the points of view of more than one character. Young writers rarely concern themselves with characterization. They do not pace their writing, with quiet passages, crescendos, climaxes. All this has to be taught.

The third problem is the one that I began this book with: the fiction that surrounds children in primary schools today is all too often, as I have suggested, 'official' fiction.

Four writers from past centuries have much to teach children. They are Robert Louis Stevenson (1850–94), Anthony Trollope (1815–82), Charles Dickens (1812–70) and Jane Austen (1775–1817). I try to show here how we can approach books by these writers through short passages. This does not mean that children shouldn't be encouraged to read whole books. I agree with Lisa Jardine (quoted in National Curriculum English, Key Stages 1–4) when she says 'A good book, studied with a good English teacher, takes you on a journey in search of answers to crucial questions in life you didn't even know you wanted (or needed) to ask.' Studying English literature is the 'biggest step towards mental freedom and independence' as Ian McEwan (quoted in the same source) puts it. This goes as much for young children as it does for older students in sixth forms and colleges. All this chapter should be read, assuming it is read at all, in the light of Kipling's remark (1928): 'Fiction is Truth's elder sister . . . No one in the world knew what truth was till somebody had told a story.'

ROBERT LOUIS STEVENSON

Stevenson was one of those authors whom I read in abridged versions. Although he is considered a children's writer, I did not discover the magic of *Treasure Island* until I read the book to my young son. I have read it to myself since several times. *Kidnapped* is a less gripping story, but it has much excitement, and some splendid villainy. Like almost all Scottish literature, it has a Calvinistic obsession with good and evil: see especially, Hogg's *Confessions of a Justified Sinner* (1824) and, more recently, Ian Rankin's Rebus detective novels. See, for a kind of distillation of this potent mix, Robert Burns' 'Holy Willie's Prayer'. The villains in Stevenson nearly always have elements of a debased religious faith. The sea captain who kidnaps David Balfour is just one example.

I read a group of children a passage from *Kidnapped*, the opening of Chapter 3. Young writers do not need to be told the whole story. Indeed, the whole story, told in an abridged form, is nothing. Stevenson's prose, on the other hand, even in short passages, is everything. The way into the book is more likely to be found on a path where the children examine, enjoy, explore such a passage. It will suggest seeds that will be planted in their minds about the power of prose. Also, playing with and thereby studying vivid passages is likely to lead to a reading of the whole novel.

The hero, David Balfour, is describing his first encounter with his uncle, of whom he has had high hopes:

There came a great rattling of chains and bolts, and the door was cautiously opened and shut again behind me as soon as I had passed.

'Go into the kitchen and touch naething' said the voice; and while the person of the house set himself to replacing the defences of the door, I groped my way forward and entered the kitchen.

The fire had burned up fairly bright, and showed me the barest room I think that I ever put my eyes on. Half a dozen dishes stood upon the shelves; the table was laid for supper with a bowl of porridge, a horn spoon, and a cup of small beer . . . There was no other thing in that great, stone-vaulted, empty chamber but lock-fast chests arranged along the wall and a corner cupboard with a padlock.

As soon as the last chain was up, the man rejoined me. He was a mean, stooping, narrow-shouldered, clay-faced creature; and his age might have been anything between fifty and seventy. His night cap was of flannel, and so was the nightgown that he wore, instead of coat and waistcoat, over his ragged shirt. He was long unshaved, but what most distressed and even daunted me, he would neither take his eyes away from me or look me fairly in the face . . .

'Ye can eat that drop parritch?'

I said I feared it was his own supper.

'O', said he. 'I can do fine wanting it. I'll take the ale though, for it slocken my cough' . . .

I sat down to the porridge with as little an appetite for meat as ever a young man had . . .

I asked the children to do the following:

- Count the words in this passage that are to do with 'chains, locks, prisons and the like'.
- Suggest some words that might describe the uncle's character as he appears here.
- Find words that tell you something about Davie's reaction to what has happened to him.
- Find references to food that suggest something about the old man.

The young writers had very little difficulty with these exercises. They readily recognized and collected the words that were about imprisonment:

rattling, chains, bolts, shut, defences, door, lock-fast, padlock, chain

They found other words that hint (and in some cases more than hint) at the old man's character:

cautiously, naething, barest, empty, mean, stooping, clay-faced, unshaved, unprofitable, cunningly

and yet other words – verbs – that describe Davie's reaction to the situation in which he finds himself:

groped, distressed, feared, daunted

It occurred to me that, because of my questioning, the children were behaving here like literary critics. I was asking these 11-year-olds to do something similar to that done by sixth formers working with a teacher. For example, he or she might be working on the first stanza of Keats' 'Ode to a Nightingale' (in Keegan, 2000).

My heart aches, and a drowsy numbness pains
   My sense, as though of hemlock I had drunk,
Or emptied some dull opiate to the drains
   One minute past, and Lethe-wards had suck:
'Tis not through envy of thy happy lot,
   But being too happy in thy happiness,
     That thou, light-winged Dryad of the trees,

> In some melodious plot
>> Of beechen green, and shadows numberless,
>> Singest of summer in full-throated ease.
>>>>>> (Keats, 1819)

I made notes about a teaching session that I witnessed. They begin:

> The teacher asks his sixth-formers to find words that are con-
> cerned with illness, pain and death, and drugs and drink. The
> resulting list leads the young critics immediately towards the
> heart of this poem: 'aches', 'drowsy', 'numbness', 'pains', 'hem-
> lock', 'drunk', 'dull', 'opiate' and 'sunk'. A search through the
> rest of the poem throws up at the very least another fifty words
> in these categories: 'draught', 'vintage', 'purple-stained', 'fever',
> 'fret', 'palsy', 'spectre-thin', and so on. The teacher asks the
> students to look closely at the sounds in these words: the effect,
> for example, of the prevalence of long consonants, and the
> rhyming: 'drunk' with 'sunk', for example.

The work the younger children were doing on the Stevenson
passage was about to help them to write – that is the main point of
this book. But it is also helping to prepare them to be critics. At the
highest level, it is helping them to be responsive, thoughtful
readers, aware of all the sounds and meanings available to writers,
and of the delicate, complex relationship between those sounds and
those meanings. At a practical level, it is schooling them in techniques that they will need later on when they face English Literature examinations.

But more importantly, the act of writing that follows this kind of
close reading, this kind of analysis of keywords, will itself make
them better critics because it is making the children active rather
than passive respondents to the passage. That is, it enables them to
respond to literature with their minds and hearts fully awake,
rather than dozing under the dull drip of a lecturer's words. It
helps them to make Stevenson's words their own. The fact that, in
their writing in response to Stevenson, they were behaving like
creative artists should not blind us to the fact that imitative creative
writing is also an act of criticism. Writing does not only create
something new; it also teaches the writer something about the
passage to which homage is being paid. Thus this kind of work
helps young people to understand texts. It should, therefore, be
more widely used in preparation for high-level work in English

Literature. This work (in the formulations of the National Curriculum English, Key Stages 1–4, p. 25) enables students to 'look for meaning beyond the literal'; 'to obtain specific information through detailed reading'; and 'to draw on . . . sound and image to obtain meaning'. They were examining how character emerges through words, not through bland description: the children recognized the miserliness in the references to food and drink and how a writer can enclose his or her readers in a certain atmosphere by the use of words that match the required atmosphere.

After I had drafted the paragraph above, I came across a book, George Steiner's *Real Presences* (1989), that made some points relevant to my argument here. He imagines a society in which the primary matters most. In our society, the secondary has taken over. In other words, the work of art (the main, primary thing) has been eclipsed in our society by criticism (the secondary thing). After a damning critique of nearly all criticism of the arts, Steiner suggests that the best criticism of a work of art is performance.

By extension, it seemed to me, children's performance of a piece of prose or a poem, and their writing while in the grip of it, constitutes criticism of a high order, as long as they are allowed to perform the prose or the poem in their own way. I would like this point to be borne in mind throughout the examples in this book: occasionally I will put in a reminder of it. I will say here merely that after reading Steiner's comments, I made all the children I met perform the poems and prose before they responded to them in writing. But that was late in the day; by then my book was nearly finished.

I read the passage from *Kidnapped* quoted above, and I suggested that the children think of a character, and write a description of a meeting with him or her:

Tears trickled down her pale cheeks. Streaks of mascara covered her nose. There was a quiet creak as I passed through the dull kitchen. Her black shawl was thrown over the back of an old rocking chair. She made an attempt to lift her head as I entered, but her will wasn't strong enough. She failed. I sensed no determination. It seemed as though she had given up. I felt sympathy as I crept closer, but my will was fading with my confidence for her.

(Sarah, 10)

PLAYING WITH TENSES

Although this next activity is not connected to the Stevenson, it seemed to a good moment to introduce it. I then showed the children the differences between the present and the past tenses. Here is the same passage worked into the present tense:

> Tears trickle down her pale cheeks. Streaks of mascara cover her nose. There is a quiet creak as I pass through the dull kitchen. Her black shawl is thrown over the back of an old rocking chair. She makes an attempt to lift her head as I enter, but her will isn't strong enough. She fails. I sense no determination. It seems as though she has given up. I feel sympathy as I creep closer, but my will is fading with my confidence for her.
>
> (Sarah, 10)

Here is another passage written during the same session – first in the past tense:

> As I walked into the gloomy room a figure stood up and slowly walked towards me. I couldn't clearly see him until he was standing right in front of me. His beady eyes, wrinkly skin and bald head gave me a strange feeling about him. He walked away from me and turned on a light. The sight was astonishing. There were knives and guns fixed along the walls. He came up to me and said, 'Are you the kid I'm supposed to be looking after?'
>
> His voice was slow, low and grumpy. I replied in a wimpy little voice, 'Yes.'
>
> 'Well, go into the kitchen and get some grub. You can 'ave some old toast from the fridge.'
>
> I walked in the kitchen. A big whiff of rotten food flew up my nose. I opened the fridge. Two rats ran out. Seven cockroaches, too. I walked back to the kidnapper from Hell, and he said, 'So where is your food?'
>
> 'I'm not hungry anymore, but thank you.'
>
> 'So are you saying my food is not good enough?'
>
> I tried to argue back but he grabbed me by the legs and chucked me in the cellar. I was all alone in the cellar. What shall I do? I thought. My parents won't be taking me home till the morning.
>
> (Natalie, 10)

And in the present tense:

> As I walk into the gloomy room a figure stands up and slowly walks towards me. I can't clearly see him until he is standing right in front of me. His beady eyes, wrinkly skin and bald head give me a strange feeling about him. He walks away from me and turns on a light. The sight is astonishing. There are knives and guns fixed along the walls. He comes up to me and says, 'Are you the kid I'm supposed to be looking after?'
>
> His voice is slow, low and grumpy. I reply in a wimpy little voice, 'Yes.'
>
> 'Well, go into the kitchen and get some grub. You can 'ave some old toast from the fridge.'
>
> I walk in the kitchen. A big whiff of rotten food flies up my nose. I open the fridge. Two rats run out. Seven cockroaches, too. I walk back to the kidnapper from Hell, and he says, 'So where is your food?'
>
> 'I'm not hungry anymore, but thank you.'
>
> 'So are you saying my food is not good enough?'
>
> I try to argue back but he grabs me by the legs and chucks me in the cellar. I am all alone in the cellar. What shall I do? My parents won't be taking me home till the morning.
>
> (Natalie, 10)

What is the effect of changing passages like these from the past into the present tense? Compare, with the young writers, these two sentences from that last piece: 'I tried to argue back but he grabbed me by the legs and chucked me in the cellar' and 'I try to argue back but he grabs me by the legs and chucks me in the cellar.' It is something about vividness and immediacy, and it is something well worth exploring. Julian Birkett (1983) gives this example from a piece of autobiographical writing by Emily Bishop and comments on the cinematic quality of the opening: 'Pre-1914 in the East End of London – drab to say the least. Two figures walking in the early morning streets . . .'

The second of Sarah's two passages certainly has a visual immediacy which the first one lacks. Later (see Chapter 5 on travel writing), I suggested that young writers use the present tense about their holidays, and there too is an immediate quality to the writing in that case. It is like a home movie.

One last example, written in the present tense:

The icy wind whips the snow in my face and my cold feet sink in the snow as I force my way through the stormy forest. The sky is overcast and the wind whistles emptily among the fir trees.

I do not notice the wooden cabin until I have almost stumbled into it. It is barely discernible, hung with icicles and covered with snow. Frost covered windows stare bleakly at me like eyeless sockets. I find the door ajar and push it open and step inside.

The room is faded, as though it is slowly dying. The floor tiles are pale and washed-out.

The walls are white and bare, and the atmosphere is as though the old cottage is remembering happier days.

A cracked sink is full of greasy plates and dirty water. Beside it is a stool. On it sits a middle-aged woman.

She has her head in her hands and appears not to have noticed me standing awkwardly in the doorway. The woman raises a weary head from worn hands and regards me with bewilderment. Her pale face has barely any expression on it. She looks as though her body is alive but her soul is dead.

(Cady, 11)

ANTHONY TROLLOPE

My next passage is from *Barchester Towers* by Anthony Trollope. Trollope is probably not a writer whom any teacher has thought suitable for children. His books are too concerned with what I will call adult politics, and the action in them is emotional rather than physical. What child would care who will be the next Bishop of Barchester? Or whether the dreadful Augustus Crosbie will turn out to be the villain adult readers suspect on first encountering him? I was well into my forties before I discovered the comedy of these books, and that sense of being involved in a high-class soap opera. But there is a moment in *Barchester Towers* – the arrival on the stage of the low-church clergyman Mr Slope – with which children can engage:

Mr Slope is tall, and not ill made. His feet and hands are large, as has ever been the case with all his family, but he has a broad chest and wide shoulders to carry off these excrescences, and on the whole his figure is good. His countenance, however, is not specially prepossessing. His hair is lank, and of a dull pale reddish hue. It is always formed into three straight lumpy masses, each brushed with admirable precision, and cemented with much grease; two of them adhere closely to the sides of his face, and the other lies at right angles above them. He wears no whiskers and is always punctiliously shaven. His face is of nearly the same colour as his hair, though perhaps a little redder: it is not unlike beef – beef, however, one would say, of a bad quality. His forehead is capacious and high, but square and heavy, and unpleasantly shining. His mouth is large, though his lips are thin and bloodless; and his big, prominent, pale brown eyes inspire anything but confidence. His nose, however, is his redeeming feature: it is pronounced, straight and well-formed; though I myself should have liked it better did it not possess a somewhat spongy, porous appearance, as though it had been cleverly formed out of a red coloured cork.

I never could endure to shake hands with Mr Slope. A cold clammy perspiration always exudes from him; and the small drops are ever to be seen standing on his brow, and his friendly grasp is unpleasant.

(Trollope, *Barchester Towers*, pp. 28–9)

While the keywords in the Stevenson passage were all about locks and keys, the keywords in the Trollope (written in the present tense) were all about (as the children readily noticed) oil, grease and dampness. One child wrote these words on the board as the children called them out while I reread the passage as oilily as I could:

cemented, grease, adhere, shining, spongy, porous, clammy, perspiration, drops

There is not much problem with the passage's diction. Another feature which is much more difficult to get across is its irony, that 'mode of speech of which the meaning is contrary to the words' (Johnson's *Dictionary*; quoted in Kemp, 1998). It is clear that Trollope doesn't mean what he says when he calls Slope 'not ill made', for example. The first time I taught this passage, the young writers in Year 6 in a large inner-city school, most of whom I had never met before, caught the essentially repellent nature of the writing, but not the irony:

She has the appearance of a sloth. She has a smell like Chanel No. 5, but five million years past its sell-by date. Her face is like a cement mixer that has dried up and broken . . . She could win a beauty contest if her opponents were dead. Her mouth is so big, it could kiss a thousand men at once. She says that she has never been in prison. True. She has been arrested twelve times though.

(Steven, 11)

Mr Scaffold is a smelly man. He works on scaffolding very hard but never has a bath afterwards. He is very short. People sometimes mistake him for a child, but I never see him apart from when I fall on his feet . . .

(Irfaan, 10)

In another school, things went differently. Here the children and staff – teachers and learning support assistants – know me well, as I had visited the school for two or three days a year for four years, and the school was a small one, less than a hundred children. Whenever I go back there, I am greeted as a friend, and my teaching methods are familiar to them: I don't have to repeat any groundwork. Also, the school is committed to readers and writers. All around the walls of the well-stocked and up-to-date library are manuscripts and illustrations by children's writers: Anthony Brown, James Mayhew, Nick Butterworth. None of the writers featured on these walls are what I have described earlier as 'official' writers. There are hundreds of photographs of writers (including myself) talking with children and teachers. This school is one of those that had stood up to OFSTED and received a rave review – despite a very low profile for the literacy hour.

I read the Trollope passage to thirty children aged from 7 to 11 – the whole Key Stage 2 group. I pointed out how Trollope speaks well of Slope: he is 'not ill made', and he has a 'broad chest and wide shoulders . . . on the whole his figure is good'; he is 'punctiliously shaven . . . his forehead is capacious and high . . . his nose is straight and well-formed' only to cut the ground away from these compliments almost immediately: 'I should have liked [his nose] better did it not possess a somewhat spongy, porous appearance'. I also noted Trollope's conversational tone.

Could the children write a description using a basic form of irony and a conversational tone?

She is fat. There is no other word for it. Fat. The next striking thing about her is her hair. It's so short! She's almost bald. Her eyes are big and bold and they are always jumping about like mental kangaroos. She's dumb. A Tots TV fan could beat her on pre-University Challenge.

Going down to her nose. It's a nice cherry nose – shame about the greasy boil on the end of it. It is so big that if you took it to the cinema it would want its own seat! Her lips are big and smothered with lipstick. She is constantly getting new boyfriends. Her last one was – ummh? – three, no four days, I think. Her shortest was 1.45 cm. – get it? Never mind.

Her shoulders are wide. Most people would associate that with being strong and a boy, you're not kidding. She once picked up three desks at one time. Unfortunately poor Tommy was on top. We never saw poor little Tommy again.

Her legs are made completely of muscle. When she runs, it looks like there are lots of millipedes inside her legs. 'Keep going, ladies!' she booms in PE.

To sum her up she (take a deep breath) is fat, lazy, strong, strict, ugly, loud, bald (almost), energetic, sarcastic, posh and clumsy.

(Rosie, 10)

No, this writer did not manage any Trollopian irony. But the lesson had helped her to write well in several other ways. Her prose is notable for a clarity (the short sentences), a broad humour (the nose requiring its own seat, and the millipedes in the legs – the passage is full of hyperbole) and a conversational style. If my objective had not been achieved, others that I had not thought of had. Here is another example from the same session:

Mr Elf has small well-formed hands. But I'd prefer them if they weren't so white and pale. He's got a strong stomach, it's true. But it's a little deformed, like a road with speed bumps. His legs are stout and short. It's OK but they are very hairy like gorillas. He'd have an attractive face if it wasn't for all the hairs with food in them. His nose has a good figure if you don't include all the warts and pus balls. His ears have a good shape but countless earwax comes out like waterfalls. His eyes are a nice blue like the sky but it would be good if they weren't glass. His mouth has big lips but it looks a bit gross when he takes his teeth out. He has a bath often, once in a century that is.

(Matthew, 10)

Again, some of the lessons of Trollope has been learned, whether or not Trollope himself would recognize the fact. Here are two further pieces by children:

Mr Carter's all right but he is unpleasantly fat and can't sit properly on a chair without falling off.

Mr Carter's all right but his eating habits are something like a two-year-old's. He always smells of rotten eggs, milky tea and mouldy cheese, and wears the same blue tee shirt which has lost nearly half the buttons.

Mr Carter's all right but his curly brown hair is tattered and needs cutting, his nose is surrounded with blue-tinged warts and huge red spots, his eyes are grey, lonely and wild and his sigh resembles a lion growling. His nails are full of grit, dirt and germs, and his trousers are stained with alcohol.

Mr Carter's all right but neighbours say he's going mad. His old house is full of dog's hair and infested with rats which have razor sharp needle teeth and long pink tails.

Mr Carter's all right but the stench of his breath is like horse muck.

But I suppose Mr Carter's all right.

(Emily, 10)

Mrs Featherby

This person I know called Mrs Featherby
is the most revolting person in the world, probably.
She's OK, quite nice you know, but really
you should have seen her.
She always wears the same old dress,
all crumpled and frayed, never been ironed
with old-fashioned pictures of flowers on it.
The jacket she wore was moth-eaten and bare
with grey mottled bobbles and holes made by
mice which lurk in her cupboard upon it.
She has a knitted tea cosy that sits on her head
to hide her mat of greasy black scrawny hairs
which to wash would feel like hell.
Her eyes are icy black, evil-looking with a slight
tingle of warm light, reassuring me she's OK.
She's a bit on the plump side with a beer gut that
sticks out like a bouncy inflatable ball.

She has started to grow a bristly moustache on the
wide gap under a fat podgy nose, which looks like
she may be a man wearing a pathetic dress.
She smells of fish and the reek of catfood and
when you go to shake her hand it is clammy, sticky
and cold with sweat.
She's OK but don't say she looks horrible
because you never know what might happen.

(Annie, 11)

The arrangement here is exactly as the writer wrote it. It seems as
though she was not sure whether she was writing prose or verse. I
do not think that Trollope or I have taught the irony. Perhaps it is
too much for children, as it is too much for journalists, who
habitually call anything coincidental or odd 'ironical'.

Later, I wrote a passage of my own, hoping to make the irony
clearer:

My aunt was all goodness. Let there be no mistake about that.

Goodness radiated from her, like the lines in a child's drawing
radiate from a star. Like the ways the fumes of petrol cover and
impregnate a street, her goodness covered and impregnated
everything it had anything to do with.

The most prominent evident part of her goodness was a
loathing of all that was evil. After all these years, I sometimes
make a table in my mind of all the evils that she loathed. It looks
like this . . .

How odd it is, by the way, to anticipate seeing this list written
down on paper. I have (I should own up) a kind of excitement at
the prospect.

Lying in bed after seven o'clock.

Drinking a second cup of tea.

Reading, on a Sunday, any book not connected with (or, quite
possibly, written by) God.

Going to the cinema.

Clearing ones throat audibly.

My aunt's face: how can I describe it? The mouth, a friend
once said, while drunk (my friend was drunk, that is, not my
aunt), like a dog's bottom. This was unkind. It was more like the
little buttons on my printer, as I observed readily, sitting now at
my desk, writing this. Her eyes were positively generous in the
attention that they gave to everyone, and everyone's actions in

her vicinity. She missed nothing. My poor Dad, for example, nipping out to the kitchen for a gulp of his home-made ale, my mother's all too evident enjoyment of chocolate cake and the music of country-and-western singers, my own breathing – smelling as it did, I am ashamed to say now, of roll-up cigarettes sucked on with my friends outside the youth club on a Saturday night. She missed none of these things.

My aunt was clever. I sometimes thought that she could be woken from a deep, God-graced slumber as I came in, not appallingly late, by the smell of Old Holborn on my mouth.

Her complexion was pale. I think she distracted the sun.

There are, of course, many other ways of following up the idea of writing prose fiction. One is to ask children to describe a room as they first encountered it. Here is an example. This writer had not, as far as I know, read the Stevenson but his teacher had taught him the same ideas: convey a character, not by saying what the person was like, but by describing his room:

The stink of stale cigarette smoke hit my face. Ashtrays blossomed foully with dog ends. Booze lingered exhaustedly in glasses here and there all around the room. I stepped across the carpet and switched off the silent television, where a woman in a smart scarlet jacket had been mouthing in front of a map of the north-east, with arrows and parallel curly lines all over it.

(Jacob, 11)

Another way of introducing a character is to concentrate on his or her clothes, and nothing else:

The first thing I noticed about her was the bright blue jacket, the bright blue short skirt. Her shoes were high-heeled. On her white blouse she wore the security badge one of the men at the gate must've given her when she came in. Her shortish blonde hair had that look that suggested that when it was out of place she had an operation on it, or even plastic surgery, rather than merely comb it. It would have taken archaeology to have done justice to the make-up: some kind of tan-coloured base, blusher or rouge or whatever it's called, and false eyelashes you could've impaled a small mouse on.

(Jenny, 11)

Another example:

> I couldn't help but notice, as she leaned over, the small insects that
> dropped like paratroopers from the sleeves of her patchy overcoat.
> They appeared to be coming from the crudely-sewn seams. The
> whole outfit reminded me of the effect you get with very old
> school plasticene – all the bright colours and neat lines gradually
> fused together into fungus like clumps of swirling, earthy brown.
> The coat showed inputs of satin, muslin, hessian and leather and
> was mottled and stained with a thousand close-to-nature inci-
> dents, that, in my neatly-laundered garments, I could only guess
> at. The coat both repulsed and awed me. It was an identity – I
> imagined shrugging its dark, damp mass onto my shoulders and
> becoming engulfed in its depth and density – a wild impulse to
> rush out with a big stick to kill squirrels, sleep in hollow tree
> trunks, and spurn shampoo. I could smell it as she sat bedside me,
> like a cave or an old, old cellar. I felt drawn to its wholeness and
> solid composition. It was her coat, and could never be anyone
> else's. Like a hunter's spear. I noticed, with some concern, that the
> feet that protruded from under it were bare and blue.
>
> (Sarah, 13)

One book on creative writing (Sellers, 1991) quotes Françoise Sagan
in its title: 'Art must take reality by surprise'. Young writers need
to be surprised too, and they can be surprised (or even astonished)
into writing imaginatively by being asked to write the end of a
novel before they have written any of the rest of the narrative.
Some were appalled by this notion in one school: 'The end? Before
you know about the people in the story? Why?' One girl took up
the challenge, though:

> He had been gone for only five minutes when John decided to go
> after him. He put on his coat and closed the door behind him.
> Then he remembered, and went back to the flat. He found
> Gerald's tape on the coffee table, picked it up and put it in his
> pocket.
>   He stood on the pavement and scanned the crowd for a friend.
> In the Saturday morning hustle, Gerald's pink bobble hat stood
> out like a beacon as he queued at one of the stalls. John smiled in
> relief and pushed towards him as fast as he could.
>   'Gerald!'
> The bobble hat turned round. John's smile broke.

The young woman looked at him.
'Oh . . . I'm sorry . . . I thought you were someone else . . .'

(Sarah, 13)

CHARLES DICKENS

The passage from Dickens that I have chosen comes from *A Christmas Carol*, Chapter 2, 'The First of Three Spirits':

> In came a fiddler with a music-book, and went up to the lofty desk, and made an orchestra of it, and tuned like fifty stomach aches. In came Mrs Fezziwig, one vast substantial smile. In came the three Miss Fezziwigs, beaming and loveable. In came the six young followers whose hearts they broke. In came all the young men and women employed in the business. In came the housemaid, with her cousin, the baker. In came the cook, with her brother's particular friend, the milkman. In came the boy from over the way . . . In they all came, one after another; some shyly, some boldly, some gracefully, some awkwardly, some pushing, some pulling; in they all came, anyhow and everyhow.

Although, as I have written, my brother had read *David Copperfield* by the time he was 14 years old, much of Dickens is too complex syntactically for most children. It is a salutary fact to me that when I read Dickens now, I am very knowledgeable about the first third of the books, and usually completely ignorant about the endings. I know all about Mr and Miss Murdstone's cruelty, and nothing at all about the death of Dora. The beginning of the book has a lovely familiarity, the end a lovely series of surprises. This is obviously evidence of my lack of staying power as a young reader.

A Christmas Carol is readily accessible to many children. The first time I taught this passage was in difficult circumstances in a school in Oxford. The writing turned out like poems. But in a low way, they were genuinely Dickensian:

In came little thieving boys
Nicking all they can.

In came a fat policeman
Getting stuck in every door.

In came their mothers
Shouting at the boys.

In came Anne-Marie
like a little baby.

(Stephen, 11)

In came a little girl from the secret garden
looking for her lovely teddy.
In came the lovely teddy
looking for the little girl.

In came the lovely teddy
with her lovely friend who
was looking for her lovely teddy
    for years and years.

(Afsama, 11)

Children make a kind of poetry even when faced with prose. Afsama's writing was scribed by a classroom assistant who was employed to work exclusively with him during the mornings.

I wrote my own account of a party with this refrain:

In comes Samantha, wearing purple velvet and a broad smile. In comes Eddie and Freddie, not for a moment taking their eyes from her, until the cakes and jelly appear on the table. In comes the timid twins, Timothy and Thomas, clutching bright presents. In comes Arabella and her aunt comes too, in case she gets into trouble. She once smashed up a party, and came home with an unsuitable boy. In comes jumping Jilly, who can't stand still, can't sit still, but who dances, dances, dances. In comes the football crowd, fresh from a game at the Rec and a scrub in the Radox bath. In comes my mother, at last, with my cake and all it's little matchstalk candles.

I then used the Dickens passage in another school, this time with 7-year-olds. I told them that they were going to have a great party, in their minds, and anybody, anybody at all, could come to it:

In came a crocodile stomping and nicking all the mince pies and eating everything. In came my best friend playing the piano and making an awful noise. In came a very famous engineer making lots of machines. He even made a new house for us. In came a very small boy and he was crying. We bought him a toy. In came a nasty man waving a dagger about. In came Mrs Richards

Incame a little girl from the secret garden
looking for her lovely teddy.
Incame the lovely teddy
looking for the little girl.

Incame the lovely teddy
with her lovely friend who
was looking for her lovely teddy
for years and years.

shouting at us because we had not done our work. In came a jazz man playing his saxophone very loudly.

(Oliver, 7)

Here are some extracts from others:

In came Mrs Lord shouting where's my dinner and getting up to dance and finding a new boyfriend.
    In came my granny smelling of manure with a gardening fork and saying 'Anyone want their garden doing?'

(Hartlie, 7)

In came Mary carrying Jesus rocking him to sleep in his blanket. In came Class 5, being the best class in the world. In came Tweety-Pie with his lady and his cage.

(John, 7)

In came my mum and dad stuffing their faces with chocolate. In came King Rameses swooping his slow legs on the floor and hitting his sarcophagus.

(Joe, 7)

In came Martha bouncy and happy, hopping on one leg and giggling. In came Jade tip-toeing quietly, hiding in the corners and whispering. In came Mr Allan trying to make his way through the children. In came Simon blasting his way in pushing and shouting and laughing. In came Helena with green hair, showing off her Simpsons hat.

(Marion, 9)

David Copperfield

My friend Duncan Bathgate, who runs one of the schools that I visit several times every year, taught some Dickens. *David Copperfield* was the Christmas production. He had based some writing with his junior class on a description of Uriah Heep in Chapter 16 of Dickens' novel. Duncan had taken the words from the Internet, and I speculated about the future of my Penguin edition of the novel and, by extension, all other books, as he told me this. The children had not actually seen a copy of the book. Samuel Johnson (in Hawkins, 1787) once complained about 'folios', big books: he preferred 'Books that you may carry to the fire, and hold readily in your hand.' Books that you take to bed, too – difficult with a screen.

It was a coincidence that the passage came from a screen, but was also, in its first sentence, about a book:

> I found Uriah reading a great fat book, with such demonstrative attention, that his lank forefinger followed up every line as he read, and made clammy tracks along the page (or so I fully believed) like a snail . . . I observed that he had not such a thing as a smile about him, and that he could only widen his mouth and make two hard creases down his cheeks, one on each side, to stand for one . . . I observed that his nostrils, which were thin and pinched, with sharp dints in them, had a singular and most uncomfortable way of expanding and contracting themselves – that they seemed to twinkle, instead of his eyes, which hardly ever twinkled at all.
>
> (Dickens, 1849–50)

The children's writing seems to have taken on much of Dickens' way of recording detail with such microscopic accuracy that the effect is bizarre: 'he could only widen his mouth and make two hard creases down his cheeks, one on each side, to stand for one' (Dickens); 'Shadows seemed to surround him and he seemed to suck in light and warmth' (Emily). This is extraordinary writing for a young child. If it feels at times to be over the top, we might reflect that Dickens' prose often feels exaggerated, as well; however, like the children, Dickens is simply looking closely at details. The children were asked to invent a character whom they could describe in Dickens' manner:

> His eyes were grey and cold and he seemed to stare through me and freeze my heart. His back was curled up and the thumb on his right hand was missing. As he wrote with his pencil, sweat dripped from his forehead and made a puddle on the floor. 'Come closer, come closer' he seemed to say as he looked at me showing me his two (and only) teeth. His hair was grey and long and damp and dirty like his eyes. Shadows seemed to surround him and he seemed to suck in light and warmth. He breathed heavily and like a mad dog panting.
>
> (Emily, 9)

His hair looks like sweaty rats' tails which have been lying in the stench of a sewer for hours on end. To touch his greasy locks would feel like the wettest oil of the sea. You could almost cook a pan of reeking bacon on them. When you go to shake his hand it feels scabby and slimy, and he has long curling fingernails with mixed up food and grits inside them. When he tries to smile he cringes horribly, showing his cheek bones.

(Annie, 10)

I sat down at the table and the vegetables covered in gravy were hanging out his mouth as he ate . . . His breath was like the smell of an expired fish.

(Anon., 9)

He eats his food in his own satisfied way, drooling between every bite. His sleeves dangle in his food, still mucky from last Sunday's lunch. His glasses are all misty, for his head is so close to the plate. He perspires like ice on a hot day.

(Anon., 10)

JANE AUSTEN

A Rettel Morf Tnua Enaj

148. *To Cassandra Esten Austen*

Wednesday 8 January 1817

Ym raed Yssac

I hsiw uoy a yppah wen raey. Ruoy xis snisuoc emac ereh yadretsey, dna dah hcae a eceip fo ekac.—Siht si elttil Yssac's yadhtrib,[1] dna ehs si eerht sraey dlo. Knarf sah nugeb gninrael Nital. Ew deef eht Nibor yreve gninrom.—Yllas netfo seriuqne retfa uoy. Yllas Mahneb sah tog a wen neerg nwog. Teirrah Thgink[2] semoc yreve yad ot daer ot Tnua Ardnassac.—Doog eyb ym raed Yssac.—Tnua Ardnassac sdnes reh tseb evol, dna os ew od lla.

Ruoy Etanoitceffa Tnua
Enaj Netsua

Notwahc, Naj: 8.
Capt: C. J. Austen RN.
22, Keppel Street
Russell Square
London

I finish with some playfulness that I found in Jane Austen (in Le Faye, 1995). I would have been pleased to have been able to teach children a passage from one of my favourite novels, *Pride and Prejudice*. I thought of that moment which, after dozens of readings, still makes me laugh out loud: Elizabeth has rejected the snobbish and foolish clergyman Mr Collins' offer of marriage, and her angry mother solicits her husband's support: 'An unhappy alternative is before you, Elizabeth', says Mr Bennet. 'From this day you must be a stranger to one of your parents. Your mother will not see you again if you do *not* marry Mr Collins, and I will never see you again if you *do*.'

But I gave up in my search. The stories are complex, the syntax often difficult and the main subject – the complicated relationship between money, love and social status – of less interest to children than it is to us. In the end I showed the children in one of the schools where the children and teachers are long-term friends of mine the letter given below, and asked the children to write a letter in an easy code. I made some suggestions. Each word could be spelt backwards as in the Austen example. They could shift each letter one or more places forward, or shift each vowel one place forward, or each consonant.

I hope that I have shown in this chapter something of what children learn as they are gripped by passages from great fiction writers (even if their first encounter has been a jokey letter). I like to think of children encountering David Balfour's Uncle Ebenezer, Obadiah Slope, Uriah Heep, the Fezziwigs and other Dickens characters in their early years, and being surprised later in life when they come across the complete novels in which these vivid people live.

After an interval, during which I am going to say more about the power of the story, I will look in Chapter 2 at children responding actively to poetry where, at least for me, the sun shines even more like Blake's Heavenly Host than it does in prose.

Tacolneston V.C. Primary School

Norwich Road

Tacolneston

Norfolk

NR16 1AL

July 12th 2000-07-12

Readi Drefi,

Uhankyoti rofi gominci oti ruoi lchoosi dnai givingi sui lali ehesti sdeaii. li tan'ci taiwi lilte eomci texni reayi ehti ynloi ghinti sii Eosire dnai ealkyrivi (Yennji) ton'wi ebi eerhi.

li khinti ymi eavouritfi tarpi foi ehti ehreti saydi sawi goindi ehti ronstemi moepi dnai ehti saikuhi dnai ehti sinquainci.

Rfteai uoyi eamci ewi ltilsi dahi nai lnusuatui keewi eecausbi Sameji Wayhemi ai raintepi mhowi ewi olsai wnoki lelwi eamci dnai ewi dahi ehti Rusi Dorlwi Lestivafi. Yopefullhi Aouisl lilwi eomci texni reayi oti eesi uoyi.

Hoi lelwi eesi uoyi texni reayi!

Eovli mrofi

        Nelehi

Xixixixi

S.Pi Shankti rofi ehti koobi!

Tacolneston v.c Primary

Norwich Road,

Tacolneston

Norfolk NR161AL

July 10th, 2000

Raed derf

Knaht uoy yrev hcum rof gnimoc ot ruo loohcs.Uoy
erew taerg ! I yllaer ekil yrteop os uoy erew taerg
rof em. I dah reven draeh fo suklah sniauqnic dna
saknat. Rof eht Muinnellim ta notsenlocat loohcs ew
dah a edarap ot eth egalliv llah. Ereht saw a etef
~~that~~ taht dah nuf semag esium dna rmaw sgodtoh. Ta
neves okcolc notsenlocat loohcs sserd pu sa soreh
morf eht tsap. I saw neeuq airotciv I dias reh etir
gniyas ew era ton desuma taht   thgin saw taerg

I yllamon od ton ekil eraepsekahs tub uoy yllaer
edam ti emoc ot efil. I nac ton tiaw litnu uoy emoc
txen raey.Taht   lliw eb ym tsal raey ta
notsenlocat loohcs dna lliw eb raey xis retfa
rebmetpes. Txen I lliw eb gniog ot thgih loohcs
lliw eb a laer egnahc. Yawyna eyb rof won.

Evol morf eerrehs

INTERVAL: MORE ON STORIES

'This is my story, this is my song' (Old hymn)

This chapter has been about prose, and about fiction in particular. It was about parts of stories: character studies, mostly ('He was a mean, stooping, narrow-shouldered, clay-faced creature') and settings ('In came . . .'). The studies were written by heroes (and one heroine) of mine: Robert Louis Stevenson, Anthony Trollope, Jane Austen and Charles Dickens.

There are the seeds of such character studies and settings in all of us, if we think about it for long enough. This is a student (me) describing a lecturer at college, for example:

> He was mad. He used to say that there must be no eccentricity in our teaching, and as he said it, he used to put his hand under his beaky nose, and as he got to 'eccentricity', he would roar the word, and sweep his hand away madly as he finished. It would be left pointing, quivering slightly, into the wings of the lecture theatre, looking like a faulty rail traffic signal, and he would stare at us, apparently utterly confident that he had made his point.

Or, there are character studies moving into short stories. This is from another student, at the same college, at the same time:

> One day, when we got back from the Hole in the Wall [a Berni Inn], where Jack had had his first taste of sherry, amontillado, his first taste of red wine (I can't remember what that was), and, dangerously, his first taste of Green Chartreuse. He had only drunk bitter beer until then. He was aggressively working class. He loved poetry . . .
>
> We found him walking round the outside of the cathedral, reciting, at the top of his voice: 'The sea is calm tonight. / The tide is full . . .'. Later, he set off the fire extinguishers in the hall of residence . . .

All of us own anecdotes like that, which we can tell when the occasion demands. Try it yourself, if possible in a group, using any one of these words as starters:

> gin, Mass, minister, virginity, driving lesson, vocation, accident, father, name, date, child

Beyond these anecdotes, there are complete stories in all our lives, in all of our memories. We tell them whenever we can: children as young as 3 years old try, often desperately, to tell them in our schools, but we stop them because 'we haven't time for that now'.

A Post-Dunblane Story

'Last night a fox came and got my ducklings. He didn't want to eat them. He just killed them.' This is a real example from a girl in an infant school in Essex. I collected it the day after Dunblane. The child was blonde and pretty. I can see her now. Her brow was furrowed with grief. She talked to me, a stranger, as she came in for registration. She told me the story, whether I wanted to hear it or not.

I have a story about that day as well:

Twenty minutes after that little girl told me about the ducklings, the headteacher took assembly. She avoided her duty to talk about the events in Scotland with the children in assembly. She had refused to talk about those events with the parents the evening before during a curriculum session about English at which I was the speaker. In assembly, all of us, teacher, child, nursery nurse, classroom assistant, were thinking about dead children lying bleeding in a primary school hall, and a dead teacher lying there too, but this headteacher wouldn't talk about any of it. I was mystified and angry ... I wondered, what had the parents thought the evening before?

Here was a story, the Dunblane one, a truly terrible one, that cried out, that wept, to be told, a story every child in the United Kingdom (and every teacher) needed to hear more than once. It was a story that the child with the duckling story was hinting at, knowingly or not. Years later, I read in the newspaper of a parent who had protected his young daughter from the news in Scotland on that awful evening, only to find out much later that she had heard the beginning of it, but not the end. She did not know that the murderer had committed suicide. She was waiting for him to come to her school and kill her and her classmates during a PE lesson ...

To lighten the atmosphere, to sweeten the palette: 'I am named after the last girlfriend my father had before he met my mother. I am Mia, she was Maria ... My mother wouldn't agree to her name, but she agreed to a slightly different version of it.' This is another real example of a story from a teacher on a course. I gathered it on my occasional pilgrimage collecting stories about names (see Sedgwick, 2000e). 'The first time I heard your father's voice, he was shouting across the parade ground' – this is my mother talking about my father. Now, of course, now that she is dead, I wish that I had listened more carefully to her stories.

None of these story-tellers – the little mourner of the ducklings, Mia, my mother – none of them would have been aware that she was telling a story: most of us aren't. But this conscious or unconscious (and definitely compulsive) story-telling is one reason why I have threaded throughout this book that part of my own story, the part that is to do with books and reading.

At the lowest level, we tell jokes, which, mostly, are nothing more or less than tiresome strategies for monopolizing the conversation. Once someone has said, 'Have you heard the one about . . .' or 'There was this bricklayer . . .' it takes a brave companion to interrupt. At a higher level, we tell stories about our holidays, or about our reactions to a television programme. At a higher level still, we talk about vital events in our lives. See, for a wonderful example, George's speech in Act Two of *Who's Afraid of Virginia Woolf?* (Albee, 1962) that begins 'When I was sixteen'.

These stories can be funny or tragic, farcical or horrific. Here is a story of mine:

I remember the birth of my son as clearly as I remember anything.

Everything is going to plan: my wife's contractions even start on the named day, 28 May 1981. Before they start, we walk the two-mile walk with which we had become familiar in the months we've been living in that then unfamiliar part of England, along a stretch of the River Gipping. I remember seeing the mallard pair whose progress we had watched: the male skinny and (as our ornithologist friend Alastair had put it) less than classic in markings, and the female albino.

I drive my wife to the hospital in our elderly red Escort. She is admitted to her little room, and I sit down next to her bed to wait, talking inconsequentially.

Then she starts convulsing, in an epileptic fit. Her lips go blue, her legs rigid and juddering. This has happened twice before. Now she is pushed on a trolley away from me. Minutes later, we can save your wife, the Australian woman doctor tells me, but not the child. They go back to her, leaving me on the stairs of the hospital.

Then they call me. Can you help? I hold her shoulders as she moans 'I don't want this to be happening', or something like that, and as a perfect little boy is born. As soon as the doctor has checked what sex he is, and that he is complete, I hold him in my arms, wrapped in whiteness, 'like a fiend hid in a cloud'. To use a jargon unknown to me then, I bond with this new human being in the opening seconds of his life . . .

Later, I wrote a poem about that birth. I challenge every teacher who is in my audience: have you not in your head and in your heart a story like that? A story that will resonate as long as you live? A story that will resonate, quite likely, as long as your children will live? Tell that story to a notebook, or to a tape recorder, leaving out feelings, just telling the facts. Here is the poem I wrote (from Sedgwick, 1986):

Ascension Day
(for Daniel)

The morning you were born
I walked the river bank,
Your slithery upward dive
Replaying and replaying
In my jumping mind
On your first day alive.

Moorhens and water-voles
Spent their neither happy
Nor unhappy lives, and
Our freakish mallard pair
Dashed to the other bank,
Homed in and waited there.

But all I could see was you,
Wrinkled nutlike and curled,
Fresh from the wash; and she,
Love, who'd pushed you through
The bewildering gap into
The swimming lit-up world.

Here the river lifts and falls
Between the trodden banks,

And then white mallards flew
Out of human reach, as
Though you had not been born
And the world wasn't new.

(28 May 1981)

I have written over fifty poems about my son. 'One day', I can imagine him saying, with Christopher Milne, son of A. A. Milne, 'I will write verses about him, and see how he likes it' (*The Times*, 22 April 1996; quoted in Kemp, 1998). All such stories are like little bits and pieces of the sun, and each one proclaims 'Holy Holy Holy . . .'. And none of them can be measured in terms of guineas, or school league tables, or National Curriculum levels.

2

Poetry the teacher

VIOLA: . . . 'tis poetical.
OLIVIA: It is the more like to be feigned . . . (*Twelfth Night*,
1:5:160)

It is probably always disastrous not to be a poet. (Lytton
Strachey, *Elizabeth and Essex*, 1928, p. 45)

INTRODUCTION

There is more in this book, later, about different forms of prose,
'fragments and broken images' such as advertisements, lists (of
rules for example), little memories of childhood (the beginnings of
autobiography), letters, travel writing. These come in Chapters 4, 5
and 7. But I have written over the past fifteen years mostly about
the teaching of poetry, the songs rather than the stories, 'Ascension
Day' rather than 'I Remember the Birth of My Son'. My real passion
is the capacity that the writing of poetry has to teach us about
ourselves, our language and our relationship with the world
around us. This mysterious process enables approaches to two
kinds of truth – the truth that is the end of an intended search, and
the truth that surprises the writer. (See my books listed in the
References for developments of this theme.)

Much of what I have written so far in this book is a response to
a challenge: can't you write something about teaching prose? I have
often felt defensive about this. I have had to admit that, in the
words of a father of a child I taught (she was writing startling
poetry) 'There's not much call for poets, is there?' There is, indeed,
little value in teaching children to be successful poets, because there
are only (at most) two or three in every generation, whether one
means successful in terms of sales (pause here for hollow laughs

from all poets) or successful in terms of reputation, or successful in being a kind of secret agent researching the truth that lies within and around us.

But we are not teaching children to help them become professional poets. Nor are we teaching children (well, we shouldn't be) in order for them to become successful dockers, or doctors, or dieticians. To teach primary school children for their possible occupations is to teach them to survive in situations that won't exist when they are grown up. And the very elements of a rigid schooling for employment – the mechanics of writing, tests, all the closing down that training implies – all of these work against what children will need when they are working: flexibility, the ability to think fast and to work with others. As George Sampson wrote: 'it is the purpose of education, not to prepare children *for* their occupations, but to prepare children *against* their occupations' (1975, his emphases).

We should teach poetry because it helps us to look at, to study the world. It enables us (if we take it and the world seriously) to see. Without its help, we are all too likely to get things wrong, seriously wrong: in Ted Hughes' (1967) phrase, we are likely 'to misunderstand the situation'. We will look at the house opposite, the trees, the hedges, the clouds floating above them and their ever-drifting, ever-changing shapes and shades and see – nothing. If we have no notion of what poetry can do, we will look at the sky ignorantly. And to be ignorant is to commit a sin. Poetry helps us to understand, helps us to a kind of innocence, helps us to understand that sun singing about holiness.

We should also teach poetry (we drop a level or two here) because it teaches us to write good prose, which possesses many of the qualities that poetry does. Poetry has, for example, concision, poise, freshness, excitement. If it doesn't, it is not poetry. This is why teaching poetry effectively teaches prose as well: can one think of good prose that is also loose, floppy, stale and dull? Above all, writers of both good prose and poetry have a rigorous alertness to the possibility of cliché, a phrase, or word, or comparison that has been over-used to the point where it is tedious. I have written before (Sedgwick, 1997, p. 59) examples that will serve again now, because it is tiresome to think up more clichés:

'Scalded cat' was once a vivid description of a response to a frightening moment, because we can have no doubt that a cat suddenly hit by boiling water will move fast; 'over the moon' conveyed excellently pleasurable, heady excitement; and news spreading 'like wildfire' encapsulated perfectly, the first time someone said it, the speed gossip has. But now, if someone used any of these phrases in a poem, except with irony, we would know they were writing when more than half-asleep.

'Cliché' is now a wider notion than merely a worn-out word or phrase. Situations and personalities can now be clichés: a school 'under siege' by OFSTED, a family 'torn apart' by a 'tart with a heart' or (that character that means so much to the tabloid press) a 'love rat'. Nevertheless, the notion of cliché puts us on the alert for what we have heard before. Awareness of a discussion about what a cliché is improves our style, because it makes us less likely to repeat tired expressions.

Two caveats: some apparent clichés are not clichés given their context. A speaker new to a language may utter commonplaces that to him or her are a statement of a truth. He or she nearly always gives them, inadvertently, a twist that makes them interesting. And, from a conservative point of view, clichés are the truth. That is why the right-wing press relies unashamedly on clichés: the past has thrown up the truth, and there is no need to think of new prose to describe the present or the future. That is why the *Daily Mail* is such a dull newspaper and why, when we glance at it in the doctors' surgery or on the train, we have that odd feeling of having read it before.

A PASSION FOR POETRY

The children quoted in Chapter 1 had had many chances for writing poems before they wrote those prose passages, and the effect of the writing of poems is visible and audible in the passages' 'concision, poise, freshness, excitement' (to use my earlier formulation), and in their avoidance of cliché.

But poetry is a personal passion for its own sake, not just for its ability to improve our writing generally. For me, it is rooted in my mother's reading and reciting poems to me when I was a child – Gray's 'Elegy in a Country Churchyard', Longfellow's 'The Slave's Dream', Goldsmith's 'The Village Smithy' – and from a love of hymns, with their simple metrics and their frank emotionalism. ('There is a fountain filled with blood / Drawn from Emmanual's veins / And sinners plunged beneath that flood / Lose all their guilty stains.') Later, this passion grew, becoming less emotional (at least on the surface) and more intellectual. I am glad that it grew and changed without weakening. The assumption that teaching, study, examination, learning would always take the magic out of poetry has always seemed sentimentally perverse to me. I think I've always wanted to *know* about poetry, as well as delight in it. Now I take it for granted that to be able to examine the way a poem works improves, rather than spoils, our relationship with it, much as an understanding (which I do not have) of how a gearbox works would improve my driving, or a knowledge of cooking (which, again, I do not have) would enhance my enjoyment of food.

The first change happened when I was taught at grammar school and at College of Education by teachers and lecturers whom I later realized had been influenced by the critic F. R. Leavis. Next, I read Leavisite criticism – Leavis himself, and his more accessible disciples like Derek Traversi and H. Coombes. These critics made me look harder at the language of poetry, and to take less for granted. In particular, they put me on the alert for sentimentality, and I looked at those old hymns again with a different eye. Indeed, I looked at some favourite poems with that different eye, as a Leavisite teacher pointed out that Gray patronized the dead in the churchyard at Stoke Poges ('mute inglorious Miltons', indeed). And as Coombes analysed with almost cruel precision a problem about the image of the sea of faith in Matthew Arnold's 'Dover Beach': the poet compares the tide to a receding religious faith, but in fact the tide comes and goes. In Arnold's poem, faith merely goes.

Then the passion for poetry grew into a conviction that it had a pedagogical function. Poetry was essentially a teacher. This was Leavisite too, though I did not know it at the time, and it looks significant to me now that one of the writers in the 1960s on children learning through the writing of poetry was a Leavisite, Denys Thompson. There is an insight partly hidden in his introduction to Clegg (1965) about poetry's pedagogical function. The rest of that book – children's writing of uncompromising vigour, and brilliant notes by Clegg – brings the insight into the open. Poetry teaches us about ourselves, the world around us, about the relationship between ourselves and the world around us, and about our language. Every poem that we either write or (possibly more importantly) *try* to write is a little research project into the similarities and differences, the tensions and affections, that exist between ourselves and everyone (and everything) else around us.

David Holbrook (without the sophistication that engagement

with OFSTED and other recent reforms has brought to current thinking about learning and education) argued the case for the teaching of poetry long ago when he wrote:

> If we know what we are doing when we teach poetry then we shall be secure; the rest of our work in English will follow by implication ... Teaching poetry is the centre of English. (Holbrook, 1961, p. 63)

Why should we believe this? The following owes much to Holbrook's argument. First, poetry is language at its most intense. Most of the famous definitions of poetry (see Sedgwick, 1997, p. 12) have this intensity somewhere embedded in them. Look at this poem by Edward Thomas:

Cock-Crow

Out of the wood of thoughts that grows by night
To be cut down by the sharp axe of light, –
Out of the night, two cocks together crow,
Cleaving the darkness with a silver blow:
And bright before my eyes twin trumpeters stand,
Heralds of splendour, one at either hand,
Each facing each as in a coat of arms:
The milkers lace their boots up at the farms.

> (Thomas, 1978, p. 81)

To make a passably good prose paraphrase of this poem, taking away as much simile and metaphor as possible, and all precision – and not being at all shy of cliché – would be very difficult, and would require many more words than the poem does. Here goes:

> From the woodland area composed of thinking that develops during the hours of sleep, to be broken up by the sharp cutting implement of brightness – out of that night two cockerels make their morning sound together, breaking night's main characteristic with a hit (?or a noised breath) made of precious stuff. And in front of me, shining, two brass instrument players are here ...

and so on. We can see the intensity of the poem, its concision, dimly, in its opposite: prose's wordy paraphrase.

Second, poetry is, amongst other things, a development of met-

aphor. It carries the reader from the concrete to the abstract, from
the known into the unknown. In its way of thus transferring
something from a familiar setting to an unfamiliar one, it is pre-
eminently educational: it is concerned with that moment between
two states of affairs: our not understanding something, and our
understanding it, at least partially. Aristotle said that metaphor
was 'the most important thing to master . . . [it] implies a perception
of resemblances'. I have written a frail poem that tries to express
this idea:

For ER

There's a place
    that, lucky,
        I get to
            sometimes. It
                separates
                    ignorance
                        and a partial
                            understanding.
                                Loneliness
                                    waits there, of
                                        course; an austere
                                            music; and
                                                a path of words
                                                    printed
                                                        without hope
                                                            across a
                                                                cold field.
                                                        (Sedgwick, 2000e)

Thus poetry, in its metaphorical behaviour, is always a link
between two apparently disparate things: between, as I have said,
the known and the unknown and also between two known things
that, before, have never been seen to be connected. It is probably
something of a cliché to say that, therefore, poetry is like an
electrical spark, jumping creatively, with effects beyond the writer's
immediate expectations and intentions. But that metaphor is the
best that I can do. Koestler talked in 1976 of a word which he
claimed to have invented – 'bisociation' – which means 'a sudden
leap of the creative imagination which connects two hitherto unre-

lated ideas'. He says that this leap works at various levels. The humblest is the pun, upon which many of the worst jokes depend of course. Higher up the hierarchy is the metaphor.

Third, poetry enables writers to communicate (National Curriculum English, Key Stages 1–4, p. 8) in the most subtle ways, both with themselves and with each other. It is concerned with getting things right, of finding the truth about things – and that is an act of communication with oneself, the primary act of communication. Who can communicate with others who cannot first communicate with him or herself? Paraphrasing the Spanish philosopher/poet Juan de Mairena (in fact, Antonio Machado working as one of his *alter egos*), poetry is an act of seeing, and thus an act of seeing truth, because the poet always believes what he can see. For a poet, there is no living without vision (this word is to be taken in its literal and in its wider sense). One never doubts, says Mairena/Machado, what one sees, only what one thinks.

Thus children who are taught to look, to have vision, will, by that token, be concerned with the truth and with searching for it. This seems to me to be immeasurably important, and is related to a matter I have been thinking about for years: Simone Weil's notion of attention, which suggests that if we look, and look with unremitting attention at something we cannot understand, though that looking seems to us to be useless, one day it will pay us back. Or as Weil gloriously says, 'it will flood like light across the soul' (Panichas, 1977).

Poetry is a process even more than it is a product. Readers of poems are accustomed, of course, to seeing poems on the page, as tangible (almost) as apples. Poets and publishers collude in the idea, understandably: books, after all, have to be made. But poetry is, even more crucially, a *process* of learning, and the idea of the *product* gets in the way of this heuristic, pedagogical notion. 'A poem is never finished, only abandoned' says Paul Valery (quoted in Auden, 1971). I think that this implies that the process of writing is more important than the product.

This is a view of education taken by the so-called progressive movement, represented by documents like the *Plowden Report*: 'if the process feels right, the product will be too' (Rosen, 1994). This line has the benefit of concentrating on what the children are, rather than what they will be when they jump the next hurdle.

POETRY – A CULTURAL DEFINITION

The oddest thing about the way poetry is perceived in our society – what one might call 'a cultural definition' of poetry – is that it is considered an art that anyone can practise without any knowledge of it. No one would consider him or herself a violinist if he or she didn't possess an instrument, have access to a teacher, and didn't habitually listen to other more experienced violinists. Similarly, someone who merely proclaimed their status as a dancer and who then capered meaninglessly across a dance floor would be, reasonably enough, an object of ridicule or, if fortunate, compassion. Everyone, on the other hand, who feels sincerely and deeply about something seems to feel a confidence (rarely shared by any reader who habitually reads poetry) that he or she is, at least for the time being, a poet. An implicit definition of poetry is that 'it is not something that I read, but something that I do' (Sedgwick, 1988). But no: 'True ease in writing comes from art, not chance, / As those move easiest who have learn'd to dance' (Alexander Pope, 'An Essay on Criticism', 1956, p. 58). 'Art' is the root of 'artificial': it is made after intense and prolonged practice. If this does not happen, poetry stops at the self-communication stage. True self-communication, and communication with the outside world, will only take place when the art is practised.

The problem is that (as Oscar Wilde said) 'all bad poetry is sincere'. Judges of poetry competitions say (you can glimpse this experience in 'The Prize-winning Poem' by Fleur Adcock in Adcock, 2000) that the lists of subjects that perennially turn up in competitions can be predicted: deaths of children and pets, the Queen, adolescent loneliness. Sincerity is not enough. Indeed, sincerity seems to go hand in hand with clichés. In a poetry competition for poems about water, which I judged many years ago, I found that water 'cascaded' everywhere, usually like 'diamonds'. Adcock noted that dawn was always heralding a bright new day, and that dew sparkles like diamonds (yes, again: diamonds are worth farthings in sincere poetry) in a dell. Pope said it all centuries ago, side-swiping on the way against obvious rhymes:

Where'er you find 'the cooling western breeze',
In the next line, it 'whispers through the trees':
If crystal streams 'with pleasing murmurs creep',
The reader's threaten'd, not in vain, with sleep.

(Pope, 1956)

To judge from my own experience, people who enter competitions often have never read poetry. So-called poems written under these circumstances are like little houses built on sand, and they collapse and die under scrutiny from anyone who actually reads poetry: poetry that is in the root sense of the word 'artificial – based on art', not bad chopped-up prose, or soppy little Patience Strong quatrains, written down as personal therapy. The necessary rock on which poems have to be built is an idea of what poetry has been in the past, and what it is now; to write about love without having read a Shakespearean or an Elizabethan lyric is a waste of time, and it is a waste of time to write about war without having read, say, Wilfred Owen or Siegfried Sassoon.

A special case of this deprivation involves children and teachers who live, learn and teach in an area famous for a poet, but who know nothing of that poet. I have worked in a school in Palmers Green, London, but none of the people in the school whom I asked had heard of their local poet, Stevie Smith; children and others in Northampton had never heard of theirs, John Clare. I wonder, when I visit Stoke Poges churchyard every summer term to work in nearby Slough schools, whether the local children know about Thomas Gray and his 'Elegy Written in a Country Churchyard', composed there. They should, if only because a few yards from Gray's grave and memorial are the graves of young people from a local school, drowned during a school trip in Cornwall.

While learning through writing is a central aim of children's writing, mere expression of personal feelings, divorced from all the poetry that has been written in previous generations, is not. It is, in the end, self-indulgence. Ezra Pound may have told us to 'make it new', but he was steeped in several classical traditions. Learning about poets who have been local to children (part of their traditions) is an especially strong way through to the roots of what poetry is, and to using poetry to help them learn. There is no contradiction between an educational view of poetry, that sees poetry as a matter of learning about oneself and one's world (not, please not, about self-expression); and a view that sees trying to write poetry as being about, necessarily, reading poetry. My book is about both.

JOHN CLARE

'Meet Me in the Green Glen'

Here is an example of children learning to write with the aid of the poet, John Clare (1793–1864). Clare was born into a barely literate family, had little education and worked as a farm labourer. He was patronized as a 'peasant poet' by fashionable literary society. When he was 44 he became insane, and died in a lunatic asylum. 'I am yet what I am none cares nor knows / My friends forsake me like a memory lost' have always struck me as two of the saddest and most beautiful lines in English verse. It is only recently, with the help of Ian Hamilton's selection of Clare's poems (1996), that I have come across more obscure work.

'Meet Me in the Green Glen' is one of Clare's late asylum poems. It reads to me like the poem of a young man, and the fact that it came late and from his utter distress seems to me to be extremely moving. It transcends the experience of the poet, beautiful as that experience apparently was, and is immediately relevant to almost all our lives:

Meet Me in the Green Glen

Love meet me in the green glen
   Beside the tall Elm tree
Where the Sweet briar smells so sweet again
   There come wi me
      Meet me in the green glen

Meet me at the sunset
   Down the green glen
Where we've often met
   By hawthorn tree and foxes den
      Meet me in the green glen

Meet me by the sheep pen
   Where briars smell at een
Meet me in the green glen
   Where whitethorn shades are green
      Meet me in the green glen

Meet me in the green glen
   By sweet briar bushes there
Meet me by your own sen

Where wild thyme blossoms fair
  Meet me in the green glen

Meet me by the sweet briar
  By the mole hill swelling there
When the west glows like a fire
  Gods crimson bed is there
    Meet me in the green glen

                                 (John Clare)

This poem provides, among with many other things, the necessary electrical leap in the last stanza with that dramatic conjunction of 'God' and 'bed'. Those 'many other things' include the music that the vowels provide, the repetition of the key phrase, and the intricate play of words to do with nature. We can, once again, help the children to be literary critics, to prepare for the days of examinations, by helping them to notice such poetic play. We can ask them to count all the vowels in the poem. We can ask them to make a list of the different sounds this vowel makes in the poem, in various combinations: 'e' (which itself makes more than one sound, of course) and 'ee' and 'ea'. There are relatively few occasions on which other vowels are used. We can ask the children to find them: the first is in 'Beside'; we can ask them to count the number of times the word 'meet' is used, and to discuss in groups the effect of the repetition of the last line in each stanza.

We can ask them to discuss, as well, the effect of the lack of punctuation in the poem. I find that it makes me read the poem in a chanting way. In pursuit of the objectives of the National Literacy Strategy, we might ask the children to copy out the poem punctu-ated. Children in cities and towns might do well to look up all the plants in the poem, and find out all they can about their shapes, colours, scents and so on. All children would move closer to making this poem their own by taking one stanza, perhaps in groups, and composing a tune for it.

I wrote an impersonation of this poem for a town setting. I think of it as a homage to Clare (and also to the Sicilian poet Salvatore Quasimodo, who ended a three-line poem *ed e subito sera*: 'and suddenly it's evening':

Meet me by McDonald's
  Near St Mary's Tower

Where wanderers with mobile
  Telephones and Walkmen
Whisper to their lovers
  Meet me by McDonald's

Meet me by the jeweller's
  Where romantics stare
At rings and precious stones
  Emeralds and rubies
Where golds on purple shine
  Meet me by the jeweller's

Meet me by the bookstall
  Where we've often met
To browse in books we couldn't buy
  Poetry and painting
Story books   Be there!
  Meet me at the bookstall

Meet me in the evening
  (Suddenly it's evening!)
After all the telephones'
  Dull demented ringing
Love come with me
  Meet me in the evening

Meet me in the Milestone
  Where we've sometimes sat
Over little glasses
  Of the cheapest wine
Buying time alone
  Meet me in the Milestone

                    (Sedgwick, in Cotton and Sedgwick, 2000)

I read the John Clare poem to children on a course for ambitious writers. I emphasized its chanting, repetitive quality, and the way the poem (as I have already mentioned) plays with the 'ee' sound: 'meet . . . me . . . green . . . tree . . . sweet . . . sweet . . . me . . . green'. We, in turn, played with the poem. I got the children to say it after me in the same tone as I had used. I then asked them to fill in missing words. These are both very traditional techniques, I reflected afterwards, but both demystify poetry: that is, they make it part of the young writers' lives, rather than a rarefied 'Grecian

Urn' experience, an experience that is only concerned with distance and romance, and with unapproachable difficulty.

I asked the children to find other tones of voice in which the poem could be said. By now, many of the children had large parts of the poem by heart. (For a discussion of the distinction between 'rote' learning and 'by heart' learning, see Sedgwick, 1999b.) I read to some of the children my poem that is modelled on 'Meet me', and I asked the children for suggestions: where could they set a 'Meet me' poem? The answers varied widely: football grounds, the solar system, shopping malls, swimming pools, the seaside, markets and in school:

Meet Me

Meet me by the Primrose Hill
(placed in a park)
where we have walked up
and run down.

Meet me by the swings
where we have had many
competitions and races.

Join me at the splash pool –
when we were young
we played all the time.

Meet me at the roundabout
where we gazed at the sky
and fixed pictures with clouds.

Meet me at the slide
where we screamed
because of the height,
where we sat scared
wondering if
we would ever make it,
where we first tasted ice cream
but dropped it on Mum's head.

Meet me at the fountain
where we took pictures
then fell in,
where we ran around

in amazement
of where the water came from.

Meet me at the top of the hill
by the stone tower
where we will suddenly
arise in total romance.

(Mariam, 11)

Meet Me

Meet me by the beach
Where the rock pools are,
Staring out to sea
Watching dolphins fly
Meet me by the beach
So we can look at shells
or even hermit crabs or other creatures too
Meet me by the beach
Where we can watch the sun set
And tread in golden sand
Meet me by the beach
And we will have a swim
And have some mintchop chip Ice cream hoping it
won't melt.

by Robert

Meet me at the....

Meet me at the fun fair,
Where the bright lights flash,
We can stay till dawn,
Meet me at the tortoise
Spinning round and round,
Meet me at the ice-cream stall
Choclate, Mint, Pistachio
We can stay till dawn,
Meet me by the roller-coaster
We'll go round and upside down,
Meet me near the tunnel of love
Where we'll go bobing up and down,
We can stay till dawn
At dawn we'll sit on the beach
Wacthing the sun rise,
We can stay till sun set.

by Rachael

Meet Me

Meet me where the highland cows roam,
where the grass smells fresh,
where the air smells sweet.

Meet me in the valley
where the heather grows,
where the silent breeze blows.

Meet me by Loch Ness
where the monster prowls
where the clouds are low.

Meet me on the mountains
up above the clouds
where the frost settles
where the slopes are steep.

Meet me in the town
where the people shop
where the people chatter.

Meet me in a log cabin
where the fire burns
and the mood is comforting.

Meet me in the forest
where the hedgehogs snuffle
where the leaves rustle.

(Sarah, 10)

Meet Me

Meet me by the coral reef
    where the angel fish swim wildly
and the sea-anemones live.

Join me in the shark's den
    where the ferocious creatures roar
and the little fish swim away in terror.

See me at the crab's place
    where they busily scurry away
and their pincers slice the sand.

Meet me at the bottom
    where the sea horse swims
and the starfish stay still.

Join me in the sea
    where the sea creatures roam
and the fishermen catch sardines.

See me in the deep sea
   where the dolphin leaps quietly
and splashes the water on the way down!

(Nadine, 11)

Some of the techniques and interests that Clare uses in his poem
have made appearances here. One of the writers has learned
something about assonance when she writes 'See me in the deep
sea'. Clare's interest in natural observation is there, too: 'where we
gazed at the sky / and fixed pictures with clouds'; 'where the frost
settles'; 'where the hedgehogs snuffle / where the leaves rustle' are
all evidence of the power to teach that Clare's poem has, of its
pedagogical function. To put it another way, the poem is heuristic.
It helps the writer learn, and it helps the reader, too.

Play is an important word here. Auden says somewhere that a
writer's first interest is not in his or her subject, as is commonly
supposed, but in the language the writer inherits. To help children
play with language – with individual words, phrases, sentences
and with whole poems – is to help them grow into adults who will
be interested in their language, and therefore, possibly, writers; and
if not writers, people who can think subtly and honestly about their
humanity.

'I Celebrate Myself'

Walt Whitman (1819–92) was an American poet who used unortho-
dox form, usually ignoring strict metre and using the line as the
rhythmic unit. He also used parallelism – a technique redolent of
the Psalms, where a sentence or statement is built up using
repeated syntactic units ('Praise ye the Lord. Praise God in his
sanctuary: praise him in the firmament of his power', Psalm 150).
Whitman was obsessed with themes that made him an attractive
figure in the 1960s: the equality of all people, especially, and, more
relevant to my purposes here, the sacredness of the self.

Sometimes, we do not need to introduce children to whole
poems. Here is a stanza from Walt Whitman's 'Song of Myself' (in
Levin, 1997):

I celebrate myself, and sing myself,
And what I assume you shall assume,
For every atom belonging to me as good belongs to you.

It is an important function of education (rarely met in mere schooling, of course) to help all children – and, indeed, all teachers – to celebrate themselves. Personal, Social and Moral Education (PSME) has, as a central plank, the idea of self-esteem. Poetry can do this best:

> I celebrate myself and sing myself
> at my extreme speed and talent
> at running down the track
> in splits of seconds,
> tearing down creating dust
> as I run
> trying to reach my goal . . .
>
> I celebrate myself, and sing myself
> for my strokes in swimming
> like a shark waiting for seals
> flipping my fins . . .
>
> I celebrate myself, and sing myself
> my talent on the piano
> feeling the keys under my fingers
> like strings helpless under the power
> of my fingers that bear such great strength.

(James, 10)

Abbie has Down's Syndrome:

> I celebrate myself, and sing myself
> my ballet dancing and my Irish dancing
> and my drama
> and my brother called John
> coming home from ballet school
> and my wonderful reading.
>
> I celebrate myself, and sing myself
> my throwing and catching with Rosemary
> and being very excited about going to a party
> and my sister Gemma and my friend Poppy both have parties
>   on Friday
> and being excellent at Guides
> and my friends playing with me.

I celebrate myself, and sing myself
that I am always very special.

(Abbie, 10)

This was done with a helper on the word processor, and read by
the child slowly and correctly to the class, who applauded. I need
not elaborate on the obvious fact: Abbie and the other children in
this class have been given by Whitman a chance to lift their self-
esteem, to celebrate themselves, to glimpse the holiness of their
hearts' affections.

THOMAS HARDY

To the Moon

'What have you looked at, Moon,
    In your time,
Now long past your prime?'
'O, I have looked at, often looked at
    Sweet, sublime,
Sore things, shudderful, night and noon
    In my time.'

'What have you mused on, Moon,
    In your day,
So aloof, so far away?'
'O, I have mused on, often mused on
    Growth, decay,
Nations alive, dead, mad, aswoon,
    In my day!'

'Have you much wondered, Moon,
    On your rounds,
Self-wrapped, beyond Earth's bounds?'
'Yea, I have wondered, often wondered
    At the sounds
Reaching me of the human tune
    On my rounds.'

'What do you think of it, Moon,
    As you go?
Is life much, or no?'
'O, I think of it, often think of it

> As a show
> God ought surely to shut up soon,
> As I go.'

This poem is typical of Hardy (1840–1928) in many ways. It has his characteristic pessimism, for a start. When I read it I think of Gabriel Oak's sheep, in *Far from the Madding Crowd*, writhing and dying under the cliff from which they have fallen and Gabriel powerless to help them; of Jude's impossible quest to become a scholar, and his inexorable decline into appalling domestic tragedy in *Jude the Obscure*; of the hopeless loves in the 'Collected Poems'. I think most of all of Hardy in the dark days of his first marriage, estranged from Emma. When she died, however, and Hardy had remarried, he raked over *Veteris vestigia flammae*, the flames of an old fire, and wrote some of the most poignant love poems in the language, for his dead wife. He remembers a moment from their courtship:

At Castle Boterel

> I look and see it there, shrinking, shrinking.
>   I look back at it amid the rain
> For the very last time; for my sand is sinking,
>   And I shall traverse old love's domain
>   Never again.

'To the Moon' is typical in its use of a complex and probably new structure: Hardy was continually inventing verse forms. It is also typical in its use of (possibly invented) evocative words, like 'shudderful'. There is a story of Hardy looking up an obscure word in the massive *Oxford Dictionary*, and finding the word had only been used once – by himself.

I read 'To the Moon' to the 8 to 11-year-old children at Bealings, one of the schools where I have a yearly date. This is one of those schools where I don't need to go over the ground. The children are ready to draft and redraft; they do not worry about spelling; they don't fuss about with erasers. They know that they have to get words down on paper in order to work on them, in order to make a poem possible. They know that, as with mathematics exams, it is important to show the working if you want to learn. The answer, the final product, is not enough.

I read the poem twice, trying to emphasize the two voices, and pointing out that there was a list in the first two stanzas: 'sweet, sublime, / Sore things, shudderful...' and 'Growth, decay, / Nations alive, dead, mad, aswoon...', and that the first list was alliterated. The children picked up on the question and answer structure, but asked about the meanings of 'sublime', 'aloof', 'mused', 'decay' and 'aswoon' (in a faint), and also asked me to explain the last two lines. All this was part of preparing children to be literary critics: to look at a poem with a view to writing one's own poem is to look closely. The activity was making them more sensitive to what a poem is, and how it is made.

I suggested that the children should write a question and answer poem, with questions addressed to the moon, the sun, a star, or a planet. (Actually, that sentence is cant: I *told* them to write a poem. It is as well that every now and then we face up to the nature of schooling. Teachers tell children to do things and, almost always, the children do them. Those of us who wear the badges of the 1960s behind our lapels – 'pleasing' displays, natural hessian, double-mounting, Joni Mitchell LPs, caftans and the rest – should remember as much as anyone the harsh nature of schools' realities. They are police states. We are, mostly, good cops.):

To the Sun

What do you hear Sun from up there?
I hear the shouts and cries of angry men,
the howl of the wolf, the bang of a gun.

What do you feel like Sun from up there?
Even though I am encircled in burning rings of fire
I feel a freezing chill of unhappiness from your earth.

What do you think Sun from up there?
I think of the world and what is to become of all the animals that
    are dying from Man's cruelty.

What do you see Sun from up there?
I see a blood-covered battlefield, a family starving and being
    ignored, even the King being betrayed.

What is the world going to come to Sun?
Nothing.

(Emily, 10)

This poem has the melodrama that children often bring to large subjects. But the picture is vividly painted, and the drama of the ending is very neatly done, when we consider that the writer could have written an overblown stanza about world endings and the like, with catastrophic explosions. The word 'Nothing' supplies a numbing shock.

The second example that I collected from this session impressed in different ways. This writer was sitting close to me as I read the poem, and could at times see it on the page. Without any hint that the children should do this, she has tried to copy Hardy's structure. The poem has two chilling phrases that are Hardyesque: 'annoys me in my peace' and 'the light in your heart dampened':

To a Star

'Why do you twinkle in the darkened sky?
        Why?'
'My light is reflected from the sun,
    The stupid, silly, shining sun
        That keeps the earth so bright and lively
        And annoys me in my peace.'

'Why do you only come out at night,
    You beautiful shining star?'
'I only come out at night because
    The sun doesn't bother to shine on me
    When the earth turns a bright pinky light,
    That's all the sun's fault.'
    'Why is the light in your heart dampened
        To hear about the sun and earth?'
    'Terrible they are, with such beauty and joy
Never think about me, a twinkling nightlight
        That brightens the darkest nights,
        If only they knew, if only they knew.'

(Annie, 10)

Another child had the moon replying to a question 'What do you see from up there?' like this: 'I see bedcovers going over bodies, mugs of cocoa beside them . . . I think they [parents, presumably] should let children stay up!' Other children showed a grasp of alliteration. The sun replies to one writer: 'Oh I have shone upon mountains / mills, milestones . . . / I have felt unhappy, untrusted / uncontrollable in my time . . .'.

The work above was done in a school I visit several times every year. The group of children I teach is never larger than twenty. In the next school, in contrast, the children didn't know me, and there were ninety of them. Again, I read the Hardy to them, but also got them saying the words: one half of them being the asker of questions, the other the moon itself. As I have said in my introduction, this is a form of criticism. For Steiner (1989) performance is the best, if not the only genuine criticism, and in performing this poem, the children were criticizing it in the sense that they were making it theirs, gaining a position in which it was possible to make valid evaluative comments on it. The first poem is notable for a dramatic ending. Originally there was a final line that went 'Crash! Bang!', but I persuaded the writer that the poem was even more dramatic without this comic-strip element. In the second poem, the writer repeats a phrase in each verse. In the third poem, I suspect that the question about bullying has a personal significance for the writer:

What is it like asteroid
hurtling around the stars and planets?
It's enjoyable, strange
and fun hurtling around them.

Asteroid asteroid what do you see
on your journey through the Milky Way?

I see black holes
exploding stars
and strange new planets.

What music, asteroid,
do you play
while hurtling round space?
I play loud and noisy music,
strange and bad.

What is it like asteroid
when you smash into planets?
You will find out soon
because it's about to happen to you!

(Christopher, 10)

Star

What do you dream about star
when shining in the sky?

I dream about, dream about
what it would be like
to shine like the sun.

How long have you been up there Star
shimmering in the sky?
I have been here, I have been here
for many years now
living and shining all day and all night.

What do you hear star
In this never-ending universe?
I hear, I hear
Nothing. Nothing at all.

(Lucy, 10)

Pluto
don't you get cold
and lonely
being the furthest away
in the solar system
and lonely in the solar system?
Wouldn't you like to be big
like Jupiter
so you are noticed more
oh Pluto?
I would love to be bigger
and noticed more.

Have you ever been bullied
by asteroids
in your lifetime Pluto?
I have been bullied
many times.

Don't you get dizzy
racing round the sun?
I do get dizzy –
wouldn't anybody?

(John, 10)

I was struck by how the children reproduced much of Hardy's mournful, pessimistic tone, and also (without their having seen the poem) something of its structure. I searched the Hardy *Collected*

Poems for other poems that might make children think and create, and came up with 'The Colour' (Hardy, 1976, p. 695), 'The Oxen' (p. 468), and 'In time of the Breaking of Nations' (p. 543). In doing this, I rediscovered Larkin's truth about Hardy (Larkin, 1983, p. 176): 'One can read him for years and years, and still be surprised.'

Finally, on the subject of Hardy, I might one day read a poem of mine that won the last prize in a *Times Educational Supplement* competition, which had asked for poems that caught the flavour of a poet, including some of their badness:

If I had walked tonight
And seen where, in satin gown,
Ghostlike, you walk the town;
And wandered the precincts where
You'd often a mind to career –

If I had walked tonight
I would dream of that wagonette;
And my face, toad-moled and wet,
Would be casting from side to side
To re-live that heart-lurching ride –

If I had walked tonight
My face, whey-shaded, slack,
My dead mind racing back . . .
But I stayed in the hearthlit gloom,
An old man's totter from your tomb.

Last Rites

I have taken the title of this section from the title of a poem by Christina Rossetti (1830–94):

Last Rites

Dead in the cold, a song-singing thrush,
Dead at the foot of a snowberry bush –
Weave him a coffin of rush,
Dig him a grave where the soft rushes grow,
Raise him a tombstone of snow.

When my son was about seven years old, his pet rabbit died. One reason children have pets at home, I think, even if we don't know this when we buy them those pets, is because the pets die. At least, that is how their parents often see the matter after the loss of the dog, or cat, or hamster, or whatever. It is better that your first bereavement is an animal, rather than Grandma or Grandad or, worse and worse and worse, a parent or a brother or sister. Animals, with their short lives, prepare us for those infinitely more terrible deaths.

Anyway, I wrote a poem for my son. I suppose I thought that my attempt at making the boy's experience into verse might strike a chord with other children:

David's Rabbit

The rabbit wasn't old
but still he's dead.
He thinks he's a dog
Auntie Alison said,
the way he would sniff
and follow you or lie
stretched out on your bed.
But now when I whisper his name
he doesn't twitch at all
and Grandad's going to bury him
by the garden shed
and I never learned how to pick him up
and now he's dead.

I read both these poems to a class of children. Again, we played with them: reading the Rossetti, for example, phrase by phrase, and then reading it again, checking that the children could supply missing words when I stopped. I could tell from their eyes as much as from their verbal responses that the poem had affected them. They looked sad, and I am sure that most of them were remembering the deaths of pets, and that the others were recalling the deaths of animals seen on television. Later, I reflected for the hundredth time on how important this sadness was; how important it was that the children should contemplate death and all its meanings while they were thinking about animals rather than human beings. Arguably, we keep animals in schools for the same reason that most of us keep animals at home: not because they live with us, but because they die.

I pointed out that the Rossetti poem was composed, thematically, of two elements: an event ('Dead in the cold . . . snowberry bush') and then a series of instructions for the mourners (the rest of the poem). I pointed out too the repetition of the word 'Dead' at the beginning of two consecutive lines.

Here are some children writing elegies for animals:

I found you Houdini
Among the leaves
Running from bush to bush.
Who did you escape from?

I bought you, Angus, in the pet shop,
Your eyes as red as rubies,
Your coat white and grey.

Houdini, your eyes were warm
As you gently nibbled my coat
Your fur grey and white.

But here I find you
Dead dead to the world.

My heart holds memories
Memories of you.
I shall bury you where the flowers grow,
Your favourite places.

(Chantal, 11)

This writer wrote 'Hodenie' for Houdini, but she understood the reference to the escapologist, by now proverbial, as my further questioning made sure. One disquieting element in the children's writing emerged as I found that, the longer their poems became, the greater the temptation to be sentimental. The Rossetti is a very short poem, and her poem is not sentimental: there is no emotion that is in excess of the facts. But 'My heart holds memories / Memories of you' embarrassed me in a mild way and I resolved, next time I taught this poem, to warn the children against this tendency, to help them to stick to the facts.

The two next writers seemed to be less sentimental. Presumably it is coincidental that they are both boys. I do not find it in my heart to argue that girls are more sentimental than boys, unless it is because their upbringing, both in the family and in wider society, bolstered by overbearing media images in entertainment and advertising, teaches them to be so:

Hamster

Lying dead in your little home,
Eyes like blackberries,
Fur like cotton,
You used to hang on the top bars
Like a little gladiator.

You were a finger-biter to my sister
But to me you were a harmless thing.
You were funny when you stuffed your cheeks.
We'll bury you in the graveyard
And everyday we'll come.

(Steven, 10)

Look at this writer's grasp of the importance of detail: the eyes like 'blackberries' of course, but also the recall of the difference of the relationship between the hamster and the writer, and the hamster and the writer's sister.

In the fields
under the trees
lies a rabbit
still bleeding.
His head is torn.
Dig a pit
in the deep damp soil
for peace.
Shine light
for its spirit to flow
ready for it to revive
in a new body
for a new journey.

(Sean, 10)

Bark Again

Her soft skin with bubbly texture and grey,
her whiskers as long as a rainbow,
I would bury her in the sunlight

where the breeze is
and the flowers grow.

I will bury her in a fine box with pearls
at the back of the garden.
I will put all her things
like carrots and toys in a box.
Please don't leave me.
You'll still be in my heart.

(Yazzmyn, 10)

I noticed how the phrase 'whiskers as long as a rainbow' caught
(with some luck? Why not? All artists need luck) the shape as well
as the length of the whiskers. I also noticed how those last two
lines were typical of how girls, who had begun with greater fluency
than the boys, who had greater attack on the task, often ended up,
nevertheless, with phrases the verbal equivalent of a comfort
blanket:

one day / just one day / I'll be there too. / (I miss my special
little friend)

and again:

I know you're up there / as an angel / flying in the sky

Next time I warned the children about this, more forcibly than
before, and in greater detail. I said something like this:

Notice how there is nothing in Christina Rossetti's poem about
her feelings. [I read the poem again.] It is all facts: 'dead ...
thrush ... bush ... coffin ... grave ... mosses ... tombstone ...
snow'. And yet – how do you think Christina felt about the
thrush? ... How does the poem make you feel? When you make
your poems, can you make sure that you don't put any feelings
in them: don't tell me what you felt, and let's see what will
happen ...

I often find it difficult to persuade teachers on courses that this is
true: that the more you suppress your feelings in writing, the more
the feelings will be evident to the reader. This is because the bare
writing allows the reader to see in the writing a possibility for

interpreting his or own feelings. Overt expression of feelings on the writer's part locks the reader into what the writer expresses. Just giving the facts frees the reader to link the story up with his or her feelings. Compare the spare ending of Hemingway's *A Farewell to Arms* (he has just seen his mistress dead in the hospital) which merely describes him walking back to the hotel 'in the rain' with the ending of the film, starring, I think, Rock Hudson. He staggers from the hospital as the rain lashes him, tears streaming between his fingers, down his face, a Rachmaninov piano concerto making sure we don't miss any point.

Here is one poem written after hearing the rabbit poem, and the Rossetti, and after hearing my warnings against emotion in excess of the facts:

> Our old cat is dead.
> Thumped by a passing car
> and he won't crawl under the fence again
> to go to the toilet in Mr Bonzo's garden.
> And he won't offer me, in the morning,
> a dead finch, or a struggling starling.
> And he won't stroke my leg
> asking me to get the tin and fork
> and scoop out his dinner . . .
> Dig a grave for our old cat
> under the fir trees
> down the end of the garden.
>
> (Jenny, 12)

In the same school I worked with another Rossetti poem, 'What Are Heavy?':

> What are Heavy? Sea-sand and sorrow.
> What are brief? Today and tomorrow.
> What are frail? Spring blossoms and youth.
> What are deep? The ocean and truth.

I pointed out that in this poem, the second parts of each answer, 'sorrow', 'tomorrow', 'youth' and 'truth', were different from the first parts, 'Sea-sand', 'Today', 'Spring blossoms' and 'The ocean'. The second were things, as I put it, that you couldn't touch. What I meant to convey was that they were abstract ideas, that they were intangible. Some of the children understood this straightaway; for others, it took a little longer. But nobody in the class failed completely to understand this idea, and to act upon it. Immediately the lines came, in the following order. The children spoke these, and I typed them on the word processor:

What is hot? Blazing sun and anger.

What is cold? Snowflakes and sadness.

What is murky? The graveyard and fog.

What is windy? Blowy wind and snow.

Then I read these lines back to the children, with plenty of justified (in my opinion) praise. Next I got the children writing:

What is funny? The clowns that smile.

What is hard? Rocks and dividing sums.

What is dark? Mist and nightmares.

What is soft? A bath and sleepiness.

What is beautiful? Flowering blossoms and life.

What is painful? A thorn and a heartbreak.

Then some of the children began to subvert the idea. This is an important element in any teaching of creative writing with older junior children:

What is purple? Vomit and jealousy.

What is evil? The devil and my sister.

What is fat? My sister and a buffalo.

Others began to experiment, after some persuasion, with other question words:

How good is technology? As good as yourself.

How do birds fly? Flap wings and go.

Are they a fright? Batman and aliens.

Eventually, we got these little four-line poems:

What is murky? The graveyard and fog.
What is fun? Playing and joy.
What is wet? The rain and tears.
What is destructive? Explosions and anger.

(Simon, 10)

What is rain? Cold and dribbly.
What is warm? Sun and breeze.
What is wet? Puddles and sea.
What do you see? Future and dreams.

(Priscilla, 9)

I like the way this next poem, written, I gathered, by a writer of whom not much was expected, grows to its thoughtful ending:

What are you? Blood, bones and skin.
What is annoying? Hard work and aches.
What is near? You and your neighbour
What is revolting? Manure and slime.

(Heidi, 9)

How does the rain fall? By clouds bursting.
How does the sea become powerful? By the moon's control.
How does the sea eat the rocks? By bashing them together and
    making sand.
How does the graveyard scare you? By funny noises around you.

(Paige, 9)

Eventually I introduced the idea of rhyme:

What is annoying? Missing the bus.
Who can sing? Nearly all of us.
What is fantastic? Playing in a pool.
What am I? I'm a silly fool.

(Savannah, 10)

EXPECTATIONS

The teacher said to me later 'I didn't think that they'd be able to do what you were asking. I thought it was too hard. But I was wrong.' Expectations in this work are everything. The fact that I did not know the children at all set me free to expect much, and I received much. The teacher, as he bravely acknowledged, had become trapped by his previous experiences of the children into expecting less than they were capable of. Research has shown that teachers often, for many reasons, trap their classes and their expectations of them in little prison cells. For example, they expect more in different subjects from one sex rather than the other. Typically, girls are expected to do better in creative writing than boys are. They expect more or less from children, making judgements according to perceptions about race; they make similar judgements, if that is not too strong a word, about social class. Connected to this, they expect more or less on the basis of clothes and even names. If we stereotype, we assume that we will get more from Edward than we will from Wayne, more from Sophie than we will from Chelsea. Any strategies that teachers develop to work against this labelling will improve the quality of children's writing.

Now, poems written after children had listened to Christopher Smart's 'For I Will Consider My Cat Jeoffry' from 'Jubilate Agno' in Keegan, 2000). I have written about children using this poem before, but I feel that this new work makes it worth printing Smart's poem again:

> For I will consider my Cat Jeoffry.
> For he is the servant of the living God, daily and duly serving him.
> For at the first glance of the glory of God in the East he worships in his way.
> For is this done by wreathing his body seven times round with elegant quickness.
> For then he leaps up to catch the musk, which is the blessing of God upon his prayer.
> For he rolls upon prank to work it in.
> For having done duty and received blessing he begins to consider himself.
> For this he performs in ten degrees.
> For first he looks upon his forepaws to see if they are clean.
> For secondly he kicks away behind to clear away there.
> For thirdly he works it upon stretch with the forepaws extended.

For fourthly he sharpens his paws by wood.
For fifthly he washes himself.
For sixthly he rolls upon wash.
For seventhly he fleas himself . . .
For eighthly he rubs himself against a post.
For ninthly he looks up for his instructions.
For tenthly he goes in quest of food . . .

Christopher Smart (1722–71) was one of those sad English poets of around this time and later (William Cowper, William Collins, John Clare) whose careers ended in madness. The Jeoffry poem was written during his illness, and to me it is as close as possible a demonstration of Dryden's truth that 'Great wits are sure to madness near alli'd, / And thin partitions do their bounds divide' ('Absalom and Achitopel' 1681, in Keegan, 2000). Samuel Johnson said of him in Boswell's *Life* (1906) [1791]: 'His infirmities were not noxious to society. He insisted upon people praying with him, and I'd as lief pray with Kit Smart as with anyone else.' I like to tell children the story of Smart's madness, and then to present this strange extract from a much longer poem as evidence of (Cowper's phrase) 'light shining out of darkness'. Here is Smart acknowledging his God and his new friend Jeoffry in haunting lines that look and sound in part like lines from the twentieth century.

Children in their own poems respond well to Smart's lines:

For I will consider the dog Prince
For first he wakes in his basket and runs upstairs.
For second he wakes his owner for his breakfast.
For third his owners open a tin of Pal and scoop it into a bowl.
For fourth he gobbles down his food and pleads for another.
For fifth he gets rejected and whines quite loudly.
For sixth my Grandad takes him for a walk in the fields and plays ball with him.
For seventh he returns panting and puffing and goes to play with his toy bone.
For eighth he gets another tin of Pal scooped into his bowl and gobbles it down.
For ninth he plays in front of the t.v. for an hour and returns to his basket.
For tenth he goes to his bone and slowly but surely falls asleep.

(Kerrie, 10)

For I will consider my mother.

For firstly on summer mornings she sits in the conservatory with her legs tucked up and the Guardian and a bowl of healthy muesli.

For secondly she looks out at the garden and says to herself I must do something about the garden today.

For thirdly she leans on the mowers, making straight lines all the way down to the fence at the bottom.

For fourthly she kneels at her little herb garden, as if she is saying her prayers.

For fifthly she feeds her rabbit with rabbit food, dandelions roots, and fills the hutch with clean straw.

For sixthly she prepares a healthy lunch for us: cheese and biscuits, lettuce, radish, tomatoes.

For seventhly we walk with her along the front at Felixstowe, stopping now and then to chuck stones into the sea.

For eighthly she buys us ice creams.

For ninthly she says, Come on back to the car, and we squash in and she drives carefully home.

For tenthly, she spends some time with her book by Margaret Atwood.

(Anon., 11)

These poems are demonstrations of Leonardo's great truth that art must be put in prison in order for it to be set free. Children do not need ideas for what to write about: they are surrounded by such ideas and, even more, those ideas are inside their hearts and their heads. What they need are not ideas, but structures in which to contain those ideas.

In my book *Writing to Learn* (2000e) I have described other lessons using classical poems: 'The Tyger' and 'I was angry with my friend' by William Blake; 'The Great Lover' by Rupert Brooke; 'To his Son' by Vincent Corbet; 'I remember, I remember' by Thomas Hood; 'Pied Beauty' by Gerard Manley Hopkins; 'Futility', 'The Chances' and 'The Dead-Beat' by Wilfred Owen; 'Riddle' by Jonathan Swift; 'If ever I should by chance grow rich' by Edward Thomas. The work described there was the seed from which the present book grew. I am sure that further study and exploration will reveal other poems that can be used by children, whether or not those poems were written with children in mind.

A mere hour that I spent with Paul Keegan's *New Penguin Book of English Verse*, published in late 2000 as I finished this book, suggested to me more poems that might be used to help children to be active critics, and to write their own poems. I draw the attention of poetry enthusiasts to Keegan, and in particular to the following:

- 'Song', p. 258 – John Suckling's advice to a discarded lover that begins 'Why so pale and wan fond Lover? / Prithee why so pale?'; children could write a poem of advice to someone who has been, as they say, 'dumped'. Teachers might refer, also, to Fleur Adcock's alarming poem, acidly explicit on this subject, 'Advice to a Discarded Lover' in Adcock, 2000.
- 'Cock Robin', p. 473; children might write a question and answer poem based on this traditional rhyme.
- Ballads, such as 'Lord Randal' on p. 578; another chance for a conversation poem.
- 'Ozymandias', by Shelley, p. 611; my friend Linda New-berry reads this sonnet to children, and then asks them to start a poem with 'I met a traveller from an antique land . . .' 'Some go for riddling ideas, some for boastfulness' she told me.

Finally, children might be challenged to write a one-line poem, like T. E. Hulme's 'Image' (1912, in Keegan, 2000):

> Old houses were scaffolding once
> and workmen whistling.

The poetry ideas described in the next chapter are to do with poems of a possibly less elevated order: parody; shape poems; poems based on syllabic counts; poems that are more everyday, more ordinary in subject. In both the present chapter and the next, however, I think that the young writers show that if they are taught by someone with an informed passion for a poem, and by the ghostly presence of the poet, that – if only for a time – the clammy hands of current statutory requirements are held back and they can exceed normal expectations. They can discover something about the truth of their imaginations, and the holiness of their heart's affections.

3

Feigning poetry

TOUCHSTONE: The truest poetry is the most feigning. (*As You Like It*, Act 3, Sc. 3)

INTRODUCTION

Alice's Adventures in Wonderland by Lewis Carroll (1832–98) was published in 1865. It is impossible to imagine its effect on contemporary readers. I am sure it was seen by some as subversive: many would have been familiar with the moral verses by Southey, Watts and others that Carroll burlesques in poems like 'You Are Old, Father William' and 'The Lobster', to take two examples. These readers would have either enjoyed or deplored Carroll's parodies. Unlike us, they would have been familiar with the originals. The only poem that Carroll pastiches that has survived better than the parody is 'Twinkle, Twinkle Little Star'.

This sense of *Alice* as subversive is difficult for us to recapture. It was a nursery book before my time, a story-time book in it, and it is a classic now. That is a dubious status, because it is harder to see the subversive truth in books that have been made ikons, that have been plinthed like a Grecian urn, or a Victorian general. We will see the truth of this with even more force in Chapter 6, where we have to deal with the classic status of Chaucer and Shakespeare. It is important for us to bear that subversiveness now in mind as we look at the book, and teach it, today.

By the middle of the twentieth century, *Alice* had lost its power to shock. Copies were in homes that contained few other books. Certainly, there were not many in our household. I remember romantic fiction by Ethel M. Dell, whose fiction I used to read surreptitiously on summer afternoons when my parents were still at work. I remember to this day a piece from one of these novels.

A couple are detained in a cottage by a storm at night. The hero is concerned not to disgrace himself by attempting to seduce the heroine and he wonders, with good reason I thought, as a new thunder-clap rolls above them: 'Were the very elements conspiring to keep them together?' I remember feeling that they probably were. I remember a passage from a book called *The Good Earth* by Pearl M. Buck, when the newly married man 'extinguishes' (what a terrifying verb) his new wife.

I remember the cream-coloured Readers' Union edition of the *War Memoirs* of Churchill (read and reread by my father, who had taken some part in that adventure, from which he didn't get back till some months after my birth, and which he never talked about). I remember a battered *Odhams Dictionary* used to help solve crosswords in the London evening paper, *The Star*; an atlas; and a set of Dickens. These were the ubiquitous blue (sometimes they're brown) hardbacks you still see today in second-hand shops, or decorating shelves in pubs with pretensions to bookishness, with the original drawings reproduced too small and an almost unreadable typeface. I binned this set last year.

I also remember a Methodist hymnbook with Gothic script, music and floppy black covers. I remember Sunday School prizes – pious biographies of doctor missionaries – and a *Collected Tennyson*. My mother would read, with evident pleasure, the opening lines of 'The Brook' ('I come from haunts of coot and hern, / I make a sudden sally / And sparkle out among the fern. / To bicker down the valley'). My brother remembers the Blackie editions of books like *The Swiss Family Robinson*, *Coral Island*, and *She* (as I do, on his jogging my memory) and he remembers reading them (as I don't). He also reminds me of an encyclopaedia sold at the door by a travelling salesman to my parents (they wanted more education for their sons, as many working-class people did, than they had had themselves because this would lead to greater prosperity). This encyclopaedia was called *The World of the Children*, and came in four dark-green hardbound volumes. I see them around in second-hand bookshops still.

Among all these books, Lewis Carroll's *Alice* was one of the most read. It was accepted by my mother, I'm glad to say, as a suitable bedtime story. It occurred to neither of us, of course, nor to my little brother, that it anticipated the modernism of the twentieth century in several ways. For example, as Benet (1973) writes with, to my ears unnecessary scepticism, that 'theorists of surrealism . . . seriously interpreted Carroll's works as early embodiments of their own principles'. Also, Alice's dream anticipates Freud's work on dreams (1900). And the verbal play of a poem like 'Jabberwocky' sounds to me as though it is behind the play of a writer like James Joyce. *Alice* is bejewelled with absurdities and ambiguities that strike chords with readers of twentieth-century fiction, and with fans of modern comedy:

> The Red Queen began again . . . 'How is bread made?'
> 'I know that!', Alice said eagerly. 'You take some flour – '
> 'Where do you pick the flower?' the White Queen asked.

For the obsessions of Freud, we need only read again these beautiful sentences:

> Alice opened the door and found that it led to a small passage, not much larger than a rat-hole: she knelt down and looked along the passage into the loveliest garden you ever saw. How she longed to get out of that dark hall, and wander about among those beds of bright flowers and those cool fountains.

CONCRETE POETRY

For my purposes here, 'Fury Said to a' (see p. 80) is a 'concrete poem' made before concrete poetry was invented. This inept term (*what* poetry? concrete *what*?) was coined in 1952 by an international group of writers in Brazil. They '[converted] words, type and white space into drawing tools' (Ron Horning in Hamilton, 1994). The idea was briefly revived in the 1960s in Britain and America, along with more successful notions like poetry and jazz. It had largely been forgotten until some old kaftan'd hippy at the National Literacy Strategy, replaying his early Bob Dylan LPs for the first time in thirty years, remembered it and foisted it, rather unkindly, on the teachers and children in primary schools throughout the country.

Despite its recent exhumation by that hippy, concrete poetry has had its day. And some of the Strategy's suggestions for shape poems are silly: 'naff little notions like concrete poetry, and thin poetry, and calligrams: "a poem about fear might be written in shaky letters to represent trembling"'. I am not going to develop my criticism of this kind of work here, because I have already done so (Sedgwick, 2000e).

"Fury said to a
mouse, That he
met in the
house,
'Let us
both go to
law: *I* will
prosecute
you. Come,
I'll take no
denial; We
must have a
trial: For
really this
morning I've
nothing
to do.'
Said the
mouse to the
cur, 'Such
a trial,
dear Sir,
With
no jury
or judge,
would be
wasting
our
breath.'
'I'll be
judge, I'll
be jury,'
said
cunning
old Fury:
'I'll
try the
whole
cause
and
condemn
you
to
death'."

But concrete poetry does have a useful function for young children because it is a creative way of using language and playing with it at the same time and, as I have already written, no one will ever be a writer who does not enjoy playing with language. In the hope that concrete poetry might have something to offer me, I have had a go in a poem about water (see p. 82) ('concrete' is spectacularly inappropriate here):

At a late stage of redrafting this chapter, I note how I can't keep the hymns of my upbringing away. I have lifted the line 'descends to the plain' from 'O Worship the King' (433 in the *English Hymnal*), where God's 'bountiful care ... / streams from the hills, / and descends to the plain'.

This is not a mere aside. We are made up of everything that has been part of us at any moment in our lives. Here I betray my old knowledge of, and affection for, hymns. Readers will find equivalent obsessions from their childhood and adolescence that they might feel embarrassed about (as I do about the hymns). The most healthy of us, mentally, are those who realize that we are made up of every thought, every feeling, every passion that we have experienced, and who accept the fact. The least healthy are those who have all too rigorously, like St Paul, 'put away childish things'.

As teachers, understanding that children come 'trailing clouds of glory' increases our ability to teach them, because that understanding makes us value their insights. Also, understanding that children come to us with the riches of a family life to back them up improves our teaching as well. As Wells (1986) and Tizard and Hughes (1984) have persuasively argued, these riches are there in all sorts of homes, not just the kind of home that teachers and the rest of the middle classes provide for their children. Wells' Rosie, identified as 'learning-disabled at school' talks all the time at home, and to great purpose. Even in what teachers typically call the 'poorest' homes, there is more purposeful learning about language going on than in the best nursery.

In contrast, assuming that children are blank slates on which it is our duty to write as much knowledge as possible before they pass out of our care into the big world, is insultingly disrespectful to what children are.

I tried another shape poem:

river

trickles

almost nothing

up high

in the

mountain's

snowy

heights

then

grows

to a steady flow

over rocks like

green pillows

under water

descends to the plain

all silt and mud silt and mud silt and mud silt and mud

moves through green

vegetation   past men with

umbrellas   coffee in flasks

and tins of maggots   then the estuary

widening   widening   widening

open sea open as sky sky

open as sea sky sea sky

A Golfing Success

one one
   one
   one
   one
   one
   o e
   o e

   o e
   o e
   one
   one
   one
   one
   one
   one
   one
   one
one one one

The children in this next class were studying water. I showed them postcard reproductions of paintings, and told them that their poems should have an appropriate shape. I also read them 'Fury Said to a Mouse' and 'A Golfing Success', a poem I treated as a riddle (more of which later):

It looks smooth
  and steady
    It looks so clear
     like a
        sea
        shell
        dropping
      into
    the
  wet
sand
    It tastes like
      tons
      of
    chocolate

```
            running
            down
            a
        sweet
    water fall
            It smells
                as
                if
                the
                    most
                beautiful
            fish
        has
    swum
  through
it
```

(Jamie, 9)

There is a marvellous shape poem in Keegan (2000):

Man's Life

Man is a Glas: Life is
A water that's weakly
walled about: sinne bring
es death: death breakes
the Glas: so runnes
the water out
finis.
(Inscription in Osmington Church, Dorset)

USING ART AS WELL AS WRITING TO PROVOKE GOOD WRITING

While I am writing about the subject of water, I note that we can use pictures from the traditions as well as poems and stories to give shape and vigour to children's writing. These poems were written while children were looking at *Seaport with the Embarkation of the Queen of Sheba* by Claude Gellee (called Claude Lorrain, 1605–82).

The water looks like
rippled silk
with tiny white highlights
scattered across the water's skin
where the sunset lies there
in a cream, green layer

(Heather, 9)

The next group of poems was written while the children and their
teacher were studying a painting from the National Gallery in
London. Nearly everybody recognizes it: *Bathers at Asnières*, by
Georges Seurat (1859–91). The subject of this picture has often been
obscured by an obsession with the pointillist technique, the manner
in which the blocks of colour have been built up by the dots made
by a paintbrush. But I wanted the children to look at the subject of
the picture. What is happening in it?

A bowler-hatted man lies on grass with a small brown dog
behind him, his left hand supporting his neck. He wears a white
shirt and dark trousers. He still has his shoes on. Boys bathe in the
water, one waist-deep, wearing a red cap. Is he drinking from the
water? The bowler-hatted man seems to be looking at this boy.
Another boy dangles his feet, as children always have done whenever water has invited them to do so. Piles of clothes, including
hats and boots, make this picture an affecting one: it could be us.
On the water, there is a boat with a man wearing a top hat, another
man punting, and someone else hidden by a white shape. Also in
this boat is a French national flag, the tricolour. In the further
distance is an oddly industrial landscape, reminding us that this is
not an idealized picture. The industrial revolution has already
altered the rural skyline near towns for ever.

The children's view of the picture was quite different from mine:

The
water looks like
shining
blue mirrors.
The
water tastes like
salty
blue coconut milk
ready to drink

                              The
                       water sounds like
                           ripples of
                        ice-cream being
                          poured into
                        ice-cream cone

                                                 (Elizabeth, 10)

     The water looks like sparkling blue ice
     The water feels like freezing cold foam.
     The water sounds like church bells ringing.

                                                 (Hannah, 9)

     Seurat Tanka

     Chattering children
     tranquil reflections of sea
     Sailing boats gliding
     Sun glittering on water
     Laughter and paddling feet.

                                                 (Sheila, 11)

The children either did not notice the threatening presence of
industry in the background of this painting or, if they did, chose to
ignore it – perhaps because they have been implicitly taught over
the years that the pastoral is poetry's true subject.

As you can see from Sheila's poem printed above, to make their
water poems the children also used some of the forms of poetry
suggested in the National Literacy Strategy. These are cinquains,
tanka and haiku. In a cinquain, the line-by-line syllable count is (or
should be) 2, 4, 6, 8, 2; in a tanka it is 5, 7, 5, 7, 7; in a haiku it is 5,
7, 5. As far as I am concerned, the purpose of these little 'prison
cells', made up of syllabic counts, is to make the children think
hard about the work that each word is doing. In their insistence on
concentration on language, on the component parts of a word, they
make the writer study the phenomenon being examined (water, in
this case) too. They increase the possibility of vision, of attention.
The next three poems are water cinquains:

                              Water
                        a still glass sheet
                       water reflects the sky

reflects the cloudy shapes on high
water

(Amy, 11)

Tranquil
Wandering ships
Deep as the universe
Mysterious majestic clouds
Ripple.

(Michael, 11)

Water
glistens slowly
beneath the gold bucket
the still liquid drips gradually
water

(Victoria, 10)

The next poem is a water tanka:

Drooling mouths cave in
Dancing waves as cold as ice
    Tug at you fiercely
Valley of death darkness flows
Like a shark, drags you under.

(Katie, 11)

INTERLUDE: A MODERN WATER POEM

A poem by Philip Larkin that I have admired since I was 18 years old is 'Water' (see *Collected Poems*, 1988). It is an uncharacteristic piece in many ways: among Larkin's largely formal, ironic, conservative, debunking, essentially English work, it is metaphysical, unrhymed, influenced by 'foreign poetry', which he suggested once he had no knowledge of or interest in. It is also daringly metaphysical in its premise, which is about constructing a religion ('I should raise in the east / A glass of water . . .'). It reminds us that, although Larkin was an agnostic, he was, as he once put it, 'an Anglican agnostic'.

I read the poem to a group of children, and asked them to imitate it. We had already been playing with the idea of water, looking closely at the paintings the children wrote about on previ-

ous pages. The poems following show that children can use literature not written for them; written, in fact, in this case, by a man
who actually disliked them:

> If I were called in
> To construct a religion
> It would be boats
> Rowing along
> The distances
> In placid waters.

(Tamara, 9)

> If I were called in
> To construct a religion
> It would start with a sprinkle of water
> The Bibles covered in ice
> The Lord's Prayer being sung
> While drinking the Lord's blood
> His body will trickle
> After swimming in a river
> If I were called in
> To construct a religion
> It will be still and tranquil

(Chris, 9)

> If I were called in
> To construct a religion
> It would be life where
> Everyday you would go
> To soak in a damp puddle
> To wash away soggy damp thoughts.

(Sophie, 10)

> If I were called in
> to construct a religion
> I should make use of sin.
>
> Going to church
> would involve an image
> of pure hatred, dancing
> on a blackened sea
> where boats would

be taken by the gods
of the second world.

The altar would be
constructed of engravings
of men discovering death
and the holy water would
be blood with a dirty
blackness at the heart.

Praising would involve
dark memories, feeling
like you have the devil
in your head.

(Sam, 11)

The process these writers are going through is hard to analyse
(especially in Sam's poem). These writings should, however,
encourage us as teachers. When children are enabled to write as
speculatively as this, to take risks with diction, to glance into
hidden corners of their consciousness, and see 'boats . . . in placid
waters' and 'Bibles covered in ice', they are, without doubt, learning, immeasurably.

BACK TO WONDERLAND: '*JABBERWOCKY*'

'very pretty . . . but . . . *rather* hard to understand!'

Back to Alice's adventures, this time through the looking glass:

'Twas brillig, and the slithy toves
  Did gyre and gimble in the wabe;
All mimsy were the borogoves,
  And the mome raths outgrabe.

'Beware the Jabberwock, my son!
  The jaws that bite, the claws that catch!
Beware the Jubjub bird, and shun
  The frumious Bandersnatch!'

He took his vorpal sword in hand:
  Long time the manxome foe he sought –
So rested he by the Tumtum tree,
  And stood awhile in thought.

And, as in uffish thought he stood,
    The Jabberwock, with eyes of flame,
Came whiffling through the tulgey wood,
    And burbled as it came!

One, two! One, two! And through and through
    The vorpal blade went snicker-snack!
He left it dead, and with its head
    He went galumphing back.

'And hast thou slain the Jabberwock?
    Come to my arms, my beamish boy!
O frabjous day! Callooh! Callay!'
    He chortled in his joy.

'Twas brillig, and the slithy toves
    Did gyre and gimble in the wabe;
All mimsy were the borogoves,
    And the mome raths outgrabe.

I asked a group of keen writers on a course to invent a nonsense-
monster, and to write a poem about it. All the poems, except one,
were failures. Some were too close to 'Jabberwocky'. Others missed
the right note by either being too nonsensical, or by being too
sensible. This next poem got it right, though. When the nonsense
threatens to tip it off balance, the writer slips in some sense. She
shows a gusto for the sounds of words, and when she read the
poem to the group, she was rewarded with a round of applause:

Kill the Swillswa

Must kill the swillswa
Kill the swillswa
Legs a-flapping eyes a-dapping
With my fundfra
With my fundfra
Kill the swillswa
Up in the pundipong tree
sits the superac swillswa
With my fundfra I climb
Up in the pundipong tree
Must kill the swillswa
Kill the swillswa
Legs a-flapping eyes a-dapping

Swish swash swirl whirl
My fundfra flies out of control
I have killed the swillswa
Killed the swillswa
Bloodstained lollo leaves still stand
But no superac swillswa

(Sarah, 10)

In another school, I saw examples of children 'translating' the first stanza of 'Jabberwocky'. What a brilliant idea this seemed. It makes the children concentrate on Carroll's nonsense diction, and thereby to see something of how the poem works; also, it teaches them the ballad metre:

'Twas boiling and the slimy toads
Did curse and holler in the wood.
All dreaded were the spiders homes
And the fish swam free.

(Ellie, 9)

'Twas chilly and the silver moon
Did shine and sparkle in the night.
All settled were the brightening stars
And the leaves drifted slow.

(Ellie, 9)

'Twas freezing and the mighty trees
Did toss and turn in the wind.
All icy were the rabbits' homes
And the mad rats ran wild.

(Philip, 9)

The last couplet in Philip's poem is genuine poetry to my ear. It speaks eloquently about disaster. I sent my friend Duncan Bathgate this idea and he sent me over fifty translations of 'Jabberwocky' from his school:

It was brilliant, and the slimy toads
Did croak and hop in the water.
All fresh were the vegetables
And the hedgehogs ran free.

(Emily, 10)

It was brilliant and the slimy bugs
Did groan in the water
And misty were the home caves . . .

(Lindsay, 8)

After reading about thirty of these poems, two negative aspects emerged. The first is that only the first stanza of Carroll's poem is suitable for this activity: in other stanzas there is not enough of his nonsense to translate, and the middle five stanzas become monotonous. The other problem is the word 'brillig', which nine times out of ten the children translate as 'brilliant'. So perhaps this was not such a brillig idea – or so I reflected as I read the fortieth version.

A possibly more creative use of this poem is to ask children to supply dictionary definitions of the nonsense words that Carroll uses. Some of the following came from sophisticated writers in the early years of secondary school:

beamish (adj.) grinning, laughing, smiling

vorpal (adj.) sharp, cutting, keen, pointed

tulgey (adj.) dark, black, grim, gloomy, murky

uffish (adj.) deep, sincere, serious, intent

slithy (adj.) slippery, slimy – whether literally or metaphorically in speech or behaviour

wabe (n.) place for enjoyment, especially near the seaside

borogove (n.) a group of boys and girls out for a good time, especially at the seaside

whiffle (vb) to move easily off the ground, like flying or gliding

frabjous (adj.) glorious, fit to be celebrated with loud music, fireworks etc

callooh (vb) to call someone from a long distance

Jubjub bird (n., ornith.) multi-coloured flightless bird that attacks humans from below while emitting cry 'jub-jub, jub-jub' from which it gets its name

frumious (adj.) sly

manxome (adj.) three-legged Minotaur-like creature living on the Isle of Man

galumph (vb) to return in triumph clumsily; to run carelessly, risking a fall

(Various writers, 8–14)

WATER BECOMING BONE: RIDDLES

Among all things wonderful –
I saw this, the most wonderful of all,
water becoming bone.

This is a free translation by Emily Roeves (unpublished) of an ancient Anglo-Saxon riddle. For a more accurate translation, see Crossley-Holland (1979). The answer is 'ice' or 'icicle'. The poem – for that is what it most definitely is – depends on a fresh perception of an ordinary event: water freezing. All poetry depends on fresh perceptions, often of ordinary things, and thus all poetry has the quality of a riddle. Poetry depends too on getting things right: 'bone' is more exact than at first appears. We understand straight away its hardness, but the colour is significant too.

I have written about riddles before many times. It will suffice to say here that an expert on riddles, Kevin Crossley-Holland (1979), has written about this form of poem: 'These misleading descriptions and mind-bending word-plays' are 'powerful because they contain secrets'. The word 'secret' is important here, because children enjoy sharing and guessing secrets. As Crossley-Holland also tells us, the word 'riddle' comes from the Anglo-Saxon 'raedan' which means to teach or instruct, and by means of jokes, puns and catch questions, a riddle teaches us about the subject of the riddle and the language in which the riddle is framed. We have playfulness and versatility in riddles too, and both of these are encouraging for children in their language work.

I met teachers on a course in Durham and, once we had got to know each other – through casual conversation at breaktimes, through more pointed conversations in the class, and (even more importantly) through their writing – I challenged them to make up riddles. They composed these in groups of two, three and four:

> I am the eternal light,
> a vibrant orange, and golden as the sun.
> I leap and pirouette
> as if I were
> the principal ballerina
> on a never-ending stage.
> I bring warmth
> like the inflamed anger
> of a person crossed
> and despatch darkness by bringing light.
> (Fire)

> I am an emerald umbrella
> opening towards the clouds.
> I leave my attire on the floor
> prior to revealing
> my new spring collection.
> My less fashion-conscious relatives
> wear the same outfit, year in, year out.
> (Tree)

> I am there the whole day through
> (unseen by you)
> drawing the face of the waves
> in the midnight sky.
> I melt like cheese
> in the morning dew.
> (Moon)

Later, I read riddles to a class of children. Some of them were by John Cotton (Cotton and Sedgwick, 1996); some were traditional examples (Crossley-Holland, 1979); some were by John Mole (from Mole 1987), and some were by Kit Wright (from Crossley-Holland and Sail, 1999). I also read some new riddles of my own:

> You take a pew
> to study my worth

while others adore
their cars in the Sabbath sun.

I have so many names,
so many natures
and quarrelling about them
you cross me time and time again.

I am not small black books in a row.
I am the silent word
walking in the garden
in the cool of the day.
(God)

Rich people have none of me,
poor people have all of me.
I am greater than God
and more wicked than the devil.
I promise you this, and I don't lie:
eat me, and you'll surely die.
(Nothing: I admit that this poem is derived from traditional
    material)

Up I step, and down
making the longest side
of a right-angled
and unlucky triangle.
Without me
you would never hold
such a high view of the world.
I am rung many times
but am nothing like a bell.
(Ladder)

A mouse I can't see
and a board of keys
decide where I go.
Sometimes when you're low
and can do nothing
mouse, keys and I are
still and silent. But
right now, right *now*, I
zig-zag up and down,
flashing amongst words,

> swooping and changing
> their order. The words
> (right *now*) begin and
> end like this: A mouse
> I can't see and a
> board of keys decide
> where I go. Sometimes.
> (Cursor)

We played with some of these riddles. I told the children that they had to guess the answer to each one. I also told them what the last word in each poem was, and insisted that they didn't try to guess the answer until I had reached that word. This kept them thinking (I hope) to the end. Certainly, a child with his or her hand waving wildly in the air is not a thinking child, is not a reasoning child, is not a learning child. He or she is a competing child, and in poetry, as Eliot said somewhere, 'is no competition'.

Riddles are not easy to teach, for two reasons. First, when the children get answers wrong, it is often because they are focusing on a single element in the poem rather than the whole poem. For example, on hearing 'I have ears' (from an unwritten riddle about corn), the children see 'head'. Most classes have to be shown that the answer to each riddle has to fit every line. Second, children often have an idea in their minds that a riddle is a joke along the lines of 'What sits in a chair and whistles?' and so on.

The best teaching of riddles depends on reading (or reciting) as many riddles as possible as clearly as possible. It should go without saying that an enthusiasm on the part of the teacher for the language of riddles (which is, to a large extent, an enthusiasm for the language of poetry) is an indispensable condition for this work. There are three rules for genuine poetry riddles. Like all rules, they are not unbreakable. But, again, like all rules, they help. They are as follows:

- The answer to the riddle should speak the riddle. In other words, the poem should either begin 'I', have 'I' somewhere in the poem, or use the word 'my' or 'me'. See nearly all the riddles quoted above.
- The riddle should almost certainly contain either a simile or a metaphor. The word 'like' is a help here, for similes. After the children grasp this idea, they can usually move

on to metaphor, where there is no 'like': the subject is simply described in terms of something else.

- It is better that the riddle should be too difficult rather than too easy. Riddles about the sun should avoid the word 'shines', for example, and riddles about rivers would be better to avoid the word 'flows'. Similarly, riddles about mirrors (a good subject) should avoid the word 'reflects'.

Unlike the teachers' examples given above, these riddles were written individually:

I fall like a dramatic rainbow.
I look above. I see the stars.
Down below I see my end, bubbling, turning.

I am blue, green, turquoise.
As I go I dodge my idols.
They stare at me as I go past.
My end draws nearer,
Nearer, nearer.

(Charlotte, 11)

The idols (originally spelled 'idles'), it turned out, were the rocks that the waterfall (the answer to the riddle) crashes past on its way down to its 'end'. But I am more interested in the fact that this writer has made a resonant poem than in the fact that she has made a successful riddle. Look at phrases like 'dramatic rainbow', 'see my end' and 'dodge my idols'. I see these as the building blocks of a genuine poem. They are fresh and resonant: phrases that, it seems to me, are quite likely never to have been written in the history of the human race.

  But I have to bear in mind that the riddle, rather than the poem, is the main thing in the writer's mind, and that the poem comes (as far as the writer can tell) by a kind of chance. Perhaps the writer does not even know that he or she is writing a poem, and often I have to make a kind of fuss of writers, pointing out the beauty, the accuracy, of what they have written. I am playing a riddle game, and he says I have written a poem!

I run steadily shaping myself differently wherever I go
Over sharp and smooth never scratching myself
    because I don't have skin.

I babble even though I cannot speak, and gurgle
    even though I have no mouth.
I follow my path wherever it may go. Making
    images of wherever I may be.
(Water)

(Rosie, 10)

I am struck by the way the lines are long, like water in a river is. I had not suggested this. I am also struck by resonant words and phrases like 'steadily shaping myself differently' (it is hard to believe that this writer had no idea of the word 'protean'), 'babble', 'gurgle' and 'making images'. I felt when I read this (the first riddle completed in this session, done in about fifteen minutes) that the request to make the poem 'difficult' had paid off.

Nobody could guess the answer to the next riddle. Children suggested 'gun' at first, then 'bomb' and so on. This piece was written out at first in prose, and the final repetition of the recurring phrase 'killing machine' – the last line – was added at my suggestion. Note the amazing puns on 'roll' and 'strike':

I am a killing machine.
I roll around.
I am a killing machine
killing everyone
who falls into my trap
everyday.
I strike and kill.
I am a killing machine.
They think I am cool
and I like that
because they fall in my trap
like that.
They sell me in stores
and I like that too.
I am a killing machine.
(Cigarette)

(Anon., 10)

I helped this writer to make his poem into short lines, but the satire was all his own; so was the pun 'roll'.

I'm with you, always.
You wear me out each day.
You ignore me, always
as if I'm not really there.
I'm ugly but I'm pretty.
I'm kind but I'm mean.
I help you always
and you never, ever say thank you.
(Life)

(Zena, 9)

The process of writing: what the children were reflecting on as they wrote these little poems was, once again, more important than the products. Processes help us to look at children as they are now.

Turn me upside down
and the top of my head
hangs by a hinge.
Old tin cans
& takeaway containers
screwed up letters
from the bank
tumble and scramble
into nowhere . . .
(Wheelie bin)

(Anon., 10)

SONG

Finally, an example from songs. I have been interested in songs since I was a teenager, and, unlike most of my friends, I was as interested in the lyrics of songs as I was in the music. I listened to the pop idols of my time, and I am sorry to say that the words of many of the songs I liked when I was 16 have adhered to the walls of my mind since then, using up space (at least as far as I see it) that would be more usefully filled by something else. I graduated, through standards by crooners like Sinatra, to the world of jazz: Billie Holiday first, then modern women singers like Cassandra Wilson, and the Brits Stacey Kent, Diana Krall and Claire Martin. I have, in the last five years, discovered classical song.

The song lyric is an important genre for children to study because, while being like a poem in various ways, it is unlike one in that it must appeal to the ear immediately, and must be married to the music and not compete with it. Also, introducing good lyrics to young children counterbalances the trite nonsense that they often have to sing in assembly. One of my favourite songs seems to meet all three of these criteria. In Cole Porter's 'You're the tops', the beloved is compared to, amongst other things, the Louvre Museum, the Tower of Pisa and Jimmy Durante's nose. I quote this song to children (I can't quote it here: the copyright laws on songs are tougher than on anything else) and I also read them a draft of a poem of mine based on it, and never finished:

Without you

my Platignum
has run out.

You are a full tray
of paperclips,
a monitor screen

that is never dark,
a printer that always works.
You are the sixty-watt bulb

in my desk lamp,
a telephone that only rings
with good news.

When you're away
my life's drawer
is a shambles

and my filing cabinet
has forgotten
its ABC

I then ask children to write a poem which mixes two elements: a grown-up person that they love: uncle, aunt, parent, teacher, and a subject that they know something about: music, perhaps, or sport, or the solar system, or animals, or food, or cars. My poem has mixed the loved one addressed in it with my study. I also tell the children that poets are often paid by the line, and I want their poem to be made up of short lines.

One boy memorably mixed his mother up with trees (he loved climbing them) and wrote 'you are / the safety net / under every branch / I stand on'. A rugby player said that his mother was 'a perfect try / right between the posts'. A car-mad boy wrote about his father: 'You are / the sparking plug / of my life', which seemed to me to be more true than he understood. Emma chose to mix her mother with food:

> You are
> the ketchup
> on my chips.
> Without you
> I'd be pizza
> without cheese
> and like a sausage roll
> with no sausage.
> When you're away
> I feel tasteless
> and like unfizzy
> lemonade.
> You are like
> a peach, your
> taste carries on
> inside but you
> never hit a
> stone.
>
> (Emma, 10)

I give the next poem exactly as it was presented to me. The writer would have been in the A set for maths (for which she had an obsession) had she been in the school with the setting system described in Chapter 4, but in C for language because her spelling was terrible and her punctuation non-existent. But what feeling there lies behind these lines, and how wrong it would be, in the face of that feeling, to concentrate on mechanical errors. The poem, she said, was addressed to her mother:

> you're my
> never ending numer
> of good things
> ading more
> evre minit
> giving all
> you can

only takeing
a way
what you
need.
Yore timesing
my happy
ness evre
second
sher-ring out
happeneness
umug us
you are a
un folld of
good ness
with follds
that never
end.

(Beth, 9)

In Sarah's poem, a somewhat disturbing picture of secondary school life emerged:

You are a crime free from minus points,
a hilarious doodle in my margin,
a lunchtime with carnage and illegal activity,
a glimpse of a hero in the dinner queue.
You are 10 out of 9,
A+,
a Walkman for my journey home, the glow of teasing first years.
You are a gullible supply teacher,
a PE lesson when it rains and we stay in,
the last day of term with no work, just card games.
You are the joy of taping rude words to the backs of sixth formers.
You are the beginning of my summer holiday.

(Sarah, 13)

A final example:

Love Poem (dedicated to my mother)

You are
The heat of Mercury

The calm drift
Of Neptune
The energy
That makes
The shattered asteroids
Rush around Saturn.

Without you
I'd be as cold
As Pluto
A dead comet
In the galaxy

You are
The wonders of Mars
You have
The knowledge of Venus
Never shrinking, always enlarging

When you are away
I'm lonely particles
In the sky

You are
The stars
Shining in the Milky Way.

When you are away
I'm as dull
As Uranus.

You are
The sun
That lights up
The whole Solar System
with love, Mariam

(Mariam, 11)

Whether feigning or not, the poems in this chapter – shape poems, poems based on syllabic count, nonsense poems, riddles, songs – all these can help us to demystify poetry. Poetry is not made up of only of Rossetti's cultivated feeling, Hardy's complicated, carpentered pessimism and Clare's beautiful invitation. It is all this nonsense – craft, some of it, and no more – given above. It, too, can help children to write. These feignings too can surprise them – and all of us – into creativity.

—4—

Fragments:
more than one kind of prose

Gather up the fragments that remain, that nothing be lost.
(St John 6:12)

INTRODUCTION

The first reason for my writing this chapter is that the world
appears to us as a broken place. The way that it works and the way
that it is ordered (assuming, of course, that it is ordered at all)
seems dislocated. However hard I try to compose my prose to
make it coherent to myself and to others (and I try hard), I must
recognize that my prose concerns a vision of a broken world.
Indeed, all art is an attempt to put the broken world in order. For
Robert Frost, poetry is a 'momentary stay against confusion', and
for the South African lawyer Albie Sachs, who fought with the
African National Congress against apartheid and who was tortured, imprisoned and eventually blown up by the South African
police (so that he lost his right arm), writing became 'a way of
organising the chaos'. (This was his casual comment on *Desert
Island Discs*, BBC Radio 4, in conversation with Sue Lawley, 26
November 2000). A book about teaching language must recognize,
not only in its argument but also in its style and its construction,
the brokenness of the world as it appears to us.

But the second reason for this chapter is to try to show that art
of the smallest, even most questionable kind ('Is this really art?' as
the *Daily Mail* has often asked) has a healing function. Kemp (1998)
quotes Sei Shonagon (c.966–c.1013): 'If writing did not exist, what
terrible depressions we should suffer from.' If someone should say,
in response to that remark, that most of the human race gets by
day by day without writing anything more than a shopping list or
a memo to a colleague, I would reply that, yes indeed, the world is

diseased with a neglect of writing. To put things in a kind of order in a notebook, however scrappily, helps us to make an object on which we can reflect, and that object takes our mind off our suffering and helps us to concentrate on what we have made, and might make of it. After a lapse of time, the object that we have made helps us to concentrate on the suffering, with less pain, and with some intent on moving on.

Even the most fragmentary art, then, possesses the power to put, if only for a moment, broken things back together. And art that is sustained and coherent is capable of making a kind of permanent sense of the darkest of our days. The German poet, Rainer Maria Rilke, wrote in a letter (*c.*1911, in Kemp, 1998): 'I don't think of work, only of gradually regaining my health through reading, rereading, reflecting.' All the more, healing is present when we try to write: see Douglas Dunn's book of poems about the death of his wife (1985) for a wonderful example. Children, unselfconsciously, try to organize the chaos – see some of the poems written in Chapter 2, where children celebrate themselves and their lives, in spite of what has happened to them. See, for example, Steven, who writes about his dead hamster 'Lying dead in your little home / Eyes like blackberries / Fur like cotton, / You used to hang on the top bars / Like a little gladiator.'

I realized in my twenties that the brokenness of the world was an apparent fact, and that the acceptance of the world as conceived by some believer as an obviously coherent whole was a sentimentality. I would have to face up to this brokenness. It crept up on me: rather slyly, I might have thought at the time. I had been taught, or told (two rather different things, as I have already suggested) that the Judaeo-Christian God was a certainty, that there were absolute moral truths surrounding, even commanding, every action. It seemed odd to me later that most of these moral truths were about marital relations, and I reflected that a Martian looking at the main Christian churches would see monolithic constructions obsessed with sex, with a side interest in the Kingdom of God. It dawned on me that, in contrast to my training at a Baptist church, nothing was certain. I came gradually to see that truth was multi-faceted, and moral truths existed only in shifting relations to each other. Becoming a relativist was a difficult process because it worked against almost all the certainties with which I had been brought up. The 'shaking of the foundations' (Paul Tillich's wonderful phrase) that occurs when a fundamentalist Baptist reads D. H. Lawrence with attention brings down mental buildings, with serious moral consequences.

The fragmentary nature of this chapter reflects the fact that we live in a century that follows one whose art was largely composed (as two contrasting poets, T. S. Eliot and Robert Graves, put it) of a heap of broken images. It was a century in which almost all the great art was fragmentary; in which the confidence of symphony-makers, oil-painters and epic poets waned, and we heard, saw and read music that troubled the ear rather than comforted it, art that could be made of anything from unmade beds to elephant dung, and poems broken, like their subject matter, into pieces, full (as in 'The Waste Land') of quotations and mandarin asides. We have discovered in the last hundred years that life is more fragmentary than it seems when we read novels written in earlier centuries, where the author's authority is godlike and unquestioned. And it is artists who have taught us this lesson.

The modernist insights of artists like Charlie Parker, Ezra Pound or Picasso are at least in part about this brokenness. These were the three of whom Larkin so despaired, for the 'modernism' that they had 'perpetrated', in his elegant, reactionary book on jazz (1970). But their insights have become old-fashioned already, with the rise of what is called 'post-modernism': involving a knowingness on the work of art about itself; about what it is up to; involving a refusal to accept that an absolute meaning in language is possible.

So this chapter itself is fragmentary. It contains fewer finished sequences of paragraphs than previous chapters, no orderly poems. I am going to try to make this chapter look a little like what it is about.

MORE ON STORIES

I have written earlier about the school notion that there is only the story to deal with. I remember this from my own primary school-days. This story is the story that, as a child, you have to write up. You have been taken, for example, on a journey, or you have been led through an experiment, or you have followed a historical project, or have seen and heard an event of some kind or other in the school hall. And then you have been asked to write 'a story about it'. The main aim of this writing was, I now suppose, to show that learning had taken place. It was a test, a record of something that, it was hoped, had been learned. It was schooling rather than education. It was, emphatically a product rather than a process. It was not intended to help learning happen.

If over the past hundred years readers have had to learn

explicitly any lessons that before were only understood implicitly (assuming that they were understood at all), it is that there is more than one kind of prose. Joyce's *Ulysses* (1922), which is a cornerstone for modernist literature, contains amongst other things conventional narrative, cod newspaper reports, dramatic dialogue, pastiche, lists (of wonderfully trivial personal expenditure), street cries ('Two apples a penny! Two for a penny!'); advertisements for potted meats; parodies of English prose styles over centuries, question and answer sequences reminiscent of the Roman catechism, quasi-obscene and quasi-blasphemous verses and, famously, an unpunctuated, half-asleep, half-awake stream of consciousness thought process by a half-asleep, half-awake, highly sexed, menstruating woman.

There is a lesson in this for us who work as teachers in whatever capacity. We've gone beyond the notion that all prose is story. But even fifteen or so years ago, we were used to only two, or possibly three kinds of prose: narrative fiction of course, reportage, and drama. Now we are more aware that children, like all of us, are surrounded by print of many kinds from their earliest years. The notion of the 'text', deriving from post-modernist thinking about language, has forced us to look critically at all sentences.

It has made us particularly critical of advertising, which has always dealt in subtleties which have only recently become evident to us. Children who are unable to read their first reading book can usually read 'McDonald's' (or just the ubiquitous 'M' symbol) or 'Burger King', and other bits and pieces of language intended to persuade them to part with their parents' money. Auden (1977) pointed out in a book review that 'children [need] to defeat propaganda of all kinds by [being aware] of which buttons are being pressed'.

My son's first reading included 'Red Lion', because that was a pub we passed frequently on a journey to the house of friends. Early passions dictated first successful reading: as a football fan at the age of 4, he could read 'Middlesbrough' and 'Darlington' before he could read anything about cats and mats, or about those noodles from the village with three corners who kept falling in puddles.

The National Curriculum says (English, Key Stage 2, p. 27) the 'range' of literature studied 'should include diaries, autobiographies, letters ... newspapers, magazines, articles, leaflets, brochures, advertisements'. National Curriculum Secondary English refers to the importance of 'non-literary texts'. The twentieth century was a pile of shattered ikons, and there is no reason to suppose the twenty-first is going to be made up of repaired certainties of the Victorian age. This chapter offers ways of working with children with these kinds of writing. Lists, advertisements in newspapers and magazines and on screen, letters, recipes, sets of rules, confessions: children can learn to be critical of all the printed detritus of modern life, and to take pleasure in it and their responses to it, whether or not their teachers are persuaded that such material is as worthy of critical attention as, say, is a Shakespeare sonnet or a paragraph of Graham Greene.

One useful aspect of the fragmentation of prose into different kinds is that it works against the notion of the canon or, in Bloom's phrase, 'the Western canon'. This is the notion that there are central texts that make an objective list of what is great. For Bloom (1994), Shakespeare ('the largest writer we will ever know ... who wrote both the best prose and the best poetry in the Western tradition') is at the centre of this canon, and he is surrounded by Dante, Chaucer, Cervantes. It is not very difficult for anyone who has studied literature at a British or American university to complete the larger part of this list. Bloom sees the deconstruction of the canon not as heuristic or exploratory – he deplores feminist, Marxist thinking that tries to interpret literature in modern terms – but as destructive.

Other critics have implicitly or explicitly presented us with canons. Brought up as a Leavisite, I was taught to dismiss the novels outside the great man's 'grand tradition' from Austen to Lawrence, and thus I never bothered to read, for example, Trollope, and E. M. Forster until much later in my life. Similarly, in poetry, writers like Housman, Auden and Larkin were simply ignored by loyal Leavisites. The negative effect of this was borne upon me when I was 33 years old and shown, for the first time, Frank O'Connor's version of an ancient Irish poem, 'What Shall We Do for Timber' (in Montague, 1974). Suddenly, and with a shocking clarity, I realized that what fine critics stated as being great often forced readers down impressive main roads where great writers lived, while writers who lived on B roads and country lanes could not be seen. Had Leavis ever read poetry post-Auden? Had he ever read O'Connor's versions of Irish work? No matter. His lofty stance was enough to make young followers dismiss such work without even looking at it.

There was a further problem for would-be writers. Obviously very, very few of us who start to write in our teens are going to be in the premier league, and the example of our great forebears, undiluted with the minor, the second-rate, is more likely to put us off writing than to encourage us. Bloom says all writers are competing with the great: Dante, Shakespeare and so on. In the context of the new writer, I cannot see what is so bad about reading the 'second-rate', if by that we mean John Fletcher, William Cowper, Anthony Trollope and A. E. Housman, as well as Shakespeare, Wordsworth, Coleridge, Dickens and T. S. Eliot.

My father must have had a sense, or maybe a hope, that his sons had bookish tendencies when he bought us, for Christmas 1958, a book called *The London Anthology* edited by Hugh and Pauline Massingham (undated). This is a strange book. A list of its contents begins:

Accidents
Actors and actresses
Air Raids
Animals and birds
Architecture
Authors
Beggars

and continues thus. You could not get more fragmented. It is a thematic anthology that seems now to be ahead of its time in that it collects together journalism, diaries, travel writing, advertisements, letters, as well as contemporary engravings, drawings and photographs. There have been similar books since. This book is the first one that came my way that was resolutely anti-canonical, and I should have carried with me to college and taken about on my journeys among the Leavisites. It would have helped me to value prose that wasn't even trying to be art; that existed because it was necessary in an everyday way, because human beings had to communicate, sell, boast, remember and persuade.

ADVERTISING

Because children are more familiar with advertising than with any other kind of writing, it is wise to introduce them to some critical work on this subject. Advertising allows for vivid, slightly over-the-top work. It also carries no threat as poetry and fiction might: all we have to do here is to be fresh, to be fun. There is an advertisement in *The London Anthology* that smells of part of Victorian London:

Dec. 7, 1846: – CATTLE SHOW. – Parties visiting this exhibition will do well ... by DINING at the BARTHOLEMEW ROOMS 308, High Holborn ... Twelve soups ready, joints, fish and poultry from 12 to 7. CHICKENS (the best) from Devonshire, 4s 6d a couple ... Dartmoor Forest or venison mutton in loins, legs, haunches or saddles; Welsh mutton in legs, haunches or saddles; Devonshire clotted cream daily; Norfolk pork sausages daily, from Mrs Coote, of Norwich; Maidstone pork sausages (with sage) daily; pork pies, from Mrs Underwood, of Leicester, from 6d to 3s each, or larger if ordered; smoked chines, Bath polonies, Hambro' sausages; Neufchatel and Buckinghamshire cream cheese; fresh laver, 10d. per lb.

This is like a found poem, that is, a set of words intended for non-literary use that works in one or more of the ways that poetry works. These words entirely lack simile, metaphor, rhyme and metre, but they do convey a rich sense of well-being. If I set the prose out like poetry, you will see what I mean:

Twelve soups ready,
joints, fish and poultry from 12 to 7.
CHICKENS (the best)
from Devonshire, 4s 6d a couple ...
Dartmoor Forest or venison mutton
in loins, legs, haunches or saddles;
Welsh mutton
in legs, haunches or saddles;
Devonshire clotted cream daily;
Norfolk pork sausages daily,
from Mrs Coote, of Norwich;
Maidstone pork sausages (with sage) daily;
pork pies,
from Mrs Underwood,
of Leicester,
from 6d to 3s each, or larger if ordered;
smoked chines,
Bath polonies,
Hambro' sausages;
Neufchatel and Buckinghamshire cream cheese;
fresh laver, 10d. per lb.

A teacher on a course wrote his advertisement for some of the food in his kitchen:

It's all strong flavours in my kitchen:
sauces first: Lea and Perrins Worcestershire,
lime pickle, bracing and sharp, to be cooked
under strong toasted cheese; Tabasco to pep up
the bland, the tame, the over-mild;
a little group of squat proud mustard soldiers
in flat yellow caps.
Then cheeses like French Camembert,
Saint Marcellin, Port Salut, Valencay;
& Italian ones smelling faintly of feet;
and English cheddar, extra mature, and Stilton
and Yarg wrapped in nettle leaves;
and anything pickled: onions and cucumber.
There's a crate of brown bottles full
of hops and malt and water:
their seductive labels promising
prize ales, bottle conditioned.
In a box on the floor
there's garlic and onions

I read this piece to children, and then asked them to write their own advertisements:

In my perfect kitchen there is
creamy mouldy looking Stilton
with blue and greenish looking veins
stinking up the air around
like your father's smelly socks.

In my perfect kitchen there is
chocolate by the ton,
sweet and melting
brown and creamy . . .

(Laura, 11)

TO START

A spicy fihieta with chillies and mince
OR
pork ribs with barbecue sauce

OR
a juicy bacon sandwich with tomato sauce
OR
a pizza with cheese-filled crust
OR
roast chicken with Cajun seasoning
OR
beef steak with onion gravy
FOLLOWED BY
lovely fresh pineapples with juice all around
OR
fresh strawberries with ice cream
WASHED DOWN WITH
lemonade all day very fizzy
milk fresh from the cow
AND THEN
coffee to wake you up

                                                        (Anon., 9)

On another occasion, I brought into a classroom a collection of advertisements – for cars, drink, records, clothes and other things that I thought would interest the children. A critical view of such material and all propaganda is a vital tool for survival in the twenty-first century. Mostly I concentrated on food and drink:

Fresh Vitamin C protection:
fresh clementines and oranges from Spain.
To have and to hold
on warm crumpets
from this day forth:
I now pronounce you
delicious on toast
[for a margarine]

Lavazza: Italian for Life.

I found one advertisement that is probably unusable in school. It is for Italian olives and tomatoes. It demonstrates the way the twentieth century left us with complex mixes of registers. Arguably, these sentences mix poetry of a debased kind, food writing (obviously) and pornography:

He gazed at her voluptuous curves in the shimmering heat of that Sicilian afternoon. How he longed to press his glistening black flesh against her firm ruby ripeness . . .

I quoted advertisements for all sorts of products that I remembered from my own life: 'Don't be vague, ask for Hague'; 'My Goodness, my Guinness'; 'Guinness is good for you'; 'You'll wonder where the yellow went when you clean your teeth with Pepsodent'; the Colgate 'ring of confidence'; 'Go to work on an egg'; 'John Collier, John Collier, the window to watch'; and, most memorably, as far as I am concerned, 'I dreamt that I went to the ball in my Maidenform bra'. I asked children to write some advertisements themselves, emphasizing the snappy quality of what I had brought in, alliteration, playfulness, simile and metaphor. Here are two extracts: 'Try the tongue-teasing taste / of my tiny chocolate toffee'; 'In my shop you will find fruit to go to play on'.

Many of the pieces the children wrote were like found poems. Nevertheless, I have to say that there is a temporary feel about much of this writing (as there is about the teacher's verses above). This is, I think, in the nature of writing that follows non-literary sources. But, like the advertisers I have quoted, the children took an opportunity to play with at least one poetic technique: alliteration. (But contrast it with the work children wrote later following their encounter with St Augustine.)

I make my muffins every Monday –
Munch them!

(Jeremy, 10)

My doughnuts are delicious:
dunk them in your drink.

(Mark, 9)

I drink chocolate hot
on cold winter holidays
when the snow has fallen.

(Alice, 9)

In my baker's shop you can buy
bacon butties
and beautiful bean burgers.

(Sophie, 9)

In my take-away you can take away
bhajees and pakoras.
In my take-away you can take away
samosas and dhall.
In my take-away you can take away
parathas.

(Raheem, 10)

As poets who have worked in advertising agencies (Peter Porter, Gavin Ewart) have found, there is much to be learned about certain poetic techniques from the less honourable art of persuasion. As I finished this book, I remembered some lines from Christina Rossetti that would enrich this work. They are from her poem 'Goblin Market'. The goblins advertise their fruit to the sisters, Laura and Lizzie:

'Come buy our orchard fruits,
Come buy, come buy:
Apples and quinces,
Lemons and oranges,
Plump unpecked cherries,
Melons and raspberries,
Bloom-down cheek peaches,
Swart-headed mulberries,
Wild free-born cranberries,
Crab-apples, dewberries,
Pine-apples, blackberries,
Apricots, strawberries; –
All ripe together
In summer weather, –

. . .

'Come buy, come buy:
Our grapes fresh from the vine,
Pomegranates full and fine,
Dates and sharp bullaces,
Rare pears and greengages,
Damsons and bilberries,
Taste them and try:
Currants and gooseberries,
Bright fire-like barberries,
Figs to fill your mouth,

Citrons from the south,
Sweet to tongue and sound to eye;
Come buy, come buy.'

(Bullace is a kind of plum, and a barberry is an oval red berry.)
This poem demonstrates again the power of the list when handled with a lust for the English language and its meanings. I will add it to the food/advertisement lesson next time I teach it.

RULES

I came across this list of rules in *The London Anthology*, p. 446–7. It is like another found poem:

> In Winter *Footballs* is a useful and charming Exercise: It is a Leather Ball about as big as ones Head, fill'd with Wind: This is kick'd about from one to t'other in the Streets, by him that can get it, and that is all the art of it.

This is by Henri Misson, and comes from his *Memoirs and Observations in his Travels over England* (1670–85). It is quoted in the Massingham *London Anthology*. Without any preparation, I asked a group of children in a remote Norfolk school to compile a list of rules for any group of people that they thought might benefit from one:

Rules for Priests

There shall be no church on Sunday or there will be a fee of
    £30,000.
No vicar shall wear a dog collar on pain of death.
There shall be no Bibles in any church or the church shall be
    made into a big pub and fined £200.
The church must be kept hot or there will be a fine of £20.
No vicar shall talk about extraordinary things out of the Bible or
    he will be crucified.

(Shane, 10)

Shane, sad-faced, a loner among the Year 6 children allowed the privilege of sitting on chairs during my assembly while the other children sat on the floor, had been a school refuser in a nearby village and was now attending mornings only at his new school.

He had scowled at me intermittently since I'd arrived, probably concerned at some new disruption to his already troubled days. I think that his problems, and his negative reaction to me as a stranger, bubble under the surface of his writing. There is something pleasingly subversive about it, anyway, and if writing (I exclude political manifestos of all kinds from this sentence) does not subvert something, it is nothing.

Rules for a Shopkeeper

If a shop-keeper eats sweets while he/she is working then they
    will never eat sweets again.
If a shop-keeper gives the wrong amount of change then he/she
    will never have any money again.
If a shop-keeper gives his/her family and friends any sweets
    free then he/she will never see her family and friends again.
If a shop-keeper talks to a friend and is ignoring the customer
    who wants to buy something then the customer gets free
    sweets for a year.
If a shop-keeper isn't in the shop when someone comes in then
    they will be sacked for life.
The shop-keeper is only allowed two cups of tea during work.

(Anon., 10)

Rules for a Norman Invader

No Norman invader shall surrender or he will be tied up with
sausages and bits of meat and tossed into a pit of scorpions and
left for a day and then pulled out and have his heart thrown in a
river.

(Anon., 10)

The session from which this work came was my first attempt with this idea, and it didn't work. This wasn't the children's fault, or their teachers, but mine. I was working in a school which I had never visited before, trying a new idea purely, almost cynically, for the sake of this book. I was unprepared. All this is not to say that the children didn't write with a quirky vividness. They did, and their teachers as well as the children, seemed to be pleased with what emerged. They also wrote a good deal – much more than one of the teachers expected (so she said). Even when an idea like this produces forced results, it does at least increase children's fluency.

But I felt that the rules idea might be feasible with more serious subjects, and with more serious thought.

I spent much time thinking about how I might develop the rules idea more successfully. About a month later, my neighbour died. He had lived for over half a century in the house opposite mine and I wrote a poem that started out as a list of rules to be observed when a neighbour is bereaved, such as be quiet, and remember him, and pray:

A Rainy Day

Rules for understanding a death in the opposite house

It will look strange: there's spaces all around it
the shape of a man we liked.
The street will be different. Unfamiliar cars will visit.
Voices will be quieter. Make yours quieter.

Remember Geoff: dressed for bowls,
cream trousers, navy blazer; tending a lawn,
smiling, crossing the road with a parcel;
pouring a drink for you, one New Year's Day.

There's the red car he bought last summer
which he was so proud of. There's the kind lady
he lived with for fifty-four years.
She has stopped crying.

As I worked on the poem, I started slowly to take the rules structure away, and some of the rules. But with the children, I kept this framework in place. I developed this idea with children in several schools: rules for welcoming a new baby seemed a possibility, and a girl in a secondary school wrote: 'Place his soft cheek against yours and whisper to him.' Judith Nichols' poem in my compilation *Jenny Kissed Me* (Sedgwick, 2000a), influenced, perhaps, by George Macbeth's poem 'Fourteen Way of Touching the Peter' (see Mackay, 1969), is a way into this lesson. I also suggested that the children might write about the welcome of a new pet. I mixed all this up with the idea of similes, taught largely through the word 'like'. I felt I had moved a long way from the less honourable beginnings in Norfolk. Before I present what the children wrote this time, a necessary digression.

SETTING: FOR AND AGAINST

In one school where the children achieved some excellent results, they were setted for Literacy. Setting does not seem to be a live issue in current books about education. I can't find index references to it in any of the books on my shelves. Not even Pollard's and Tann's practically encyclopaedic *Reflective Teaching in the Primary School* (1987) mentions it. This may well be because writers who were interested in childhood stopped writing about streaming and setting on the false (and over-optimistic) assumption that the argument had, politically, been won as, indeed, it had been won intellectually; that this unfair practice would never come back again.

But it has! I think it is worth putting down again here the case against this arrangement. It had all but disappeared by the late 1970s, but pressure put on teachers by successive legislation has revived it because, presumably, it is easier to teach to tests when the children are seen to be of about the same ability. It is, in other words, an administrative rather than an educational matter: schools who set for literacy and mathematics are likely to obtain better status in league tables. But, educationally, setting teaches children volumes about their teachers' expectations. What am I supposed to do if I am in Set A? What am I supposed to do if I am in Set C? This may be satisfactory for the A set (though I don't think it does much for their respect for the other children). It is wrong for the children in the other sets, especially, of course, C, to be implicitly told that the expectations the school has of them are so low that they cannot be taught with their peers.

The children in the Essex junior school where I tried the rules idea for the second time were setted for English. When I started teaching the children in Year 5, they were sitting together – ninety-odd of them – in a carpeted area. Doors to three classrooms led off from this area. As I sent them off to write the rules poems I assumed that they would be going to their normal classrooms, but one of the teachers called out 'literacy groups!' (which is the modern version of 'English sets!'). The children went to rooms that were not, it turned out, their form rooms but to rooms that they used for any work concerned with language. I wondered whether the teachers believed that the children did not know that they were being sorted out in terms of their perceived intellectual status.

The atmosphere in the three sets (I noted furtively) is quite different: 'Children in C and B would benefit from some of the pacy, hothouse feel in A, especially if the children were engaged in collaborative writing.' I noted also that I was 'deprived of an option'. There is an option in my teaching that I always find useful. When the children have been writing for about fifteen minutes, I always have a quick plenary session when the children who wish to do so can read lines that they have written and with which they are pleased. This has two effects. First, the children who read out something that they have written receive encouragement from their teachers and their peers. They also receive intense listening, at the least, and often a round of applause (though, of course, in the long term, the intense listening is far more valuable than the clapping). Second, children think about what they and their colleagues have written. Children who listen learn something from what they hear from the readers, and can adapt it for their own writing. This plenary session is a time in classrooms that is more valuable than I could have dreamt of when I was a young teacher. Unmeasurable learning happens, as children (and, I hope, teachers) concentrate.

In the setted classrooms this plenary was more difficult. The abler writers were deprived of the chance of teaching the other children, and the less able were deprived of the chance of being taught by children who were, quite likely, more able writers than their teachers, given that their ability was still mixed with unselfconsciousness.

Finally, I reflected afterwards, setting is wrong simply because it labels children. I work in one town that still uses the 11+. To put it baldly, if you wear black and white on schooldays in this town, you are a failure; if you wear maroon and blue, you are a success. That labelling seems to me to be a sign of disrespect for the students, and so does the labelling implicit in setting.

The atmosphere in each of the three rooms was so different. If I can try to think about why, I think in terms of social class. The third set was largely filled with boys with close-cropped hair, with girls wearing sub-Spice Girls uniforms. The top set was full of children, self-possessed and sure of themselves. If the human race has to be divided in terms of ability, class or whatever, should it start in the primary school? I am sure that this is an immoral idea.

Defending her practice, the headteacher said to me:

It was here when I came and there was no way that I could have dismantled it. We only do it in Years 5 and 6. And it works. It allows the lower ability children to be stretched in smaller groups, it improves behaviour – there is a significant improvement between Years 4 and 5 when the less able are setted. I worked in a special school, and it is a similar argument: children working with other children of similar ability don't get the mickey taken so much. They're happier with their own ability, they don't feel inadequate. Sometimes the children move between sets; we're quite flexible.

I asked the headteacher where her strongest teachers were, and whether any children were in Set A for Maths but Set C for English, and vice versa:

> I have the strongest teachers mostly in the middle set, because they're the crux, they're where they might get on to level 4 . . . about one child in any given year is in top for maths and bottom for English, no more than that.

I could see the force of the headteacher's argument. I have never had to run a school with political pressure on me all the time to raise children to different levels. But I am an unreformed liberal with a sixties background, and not setting goes with non-uniform policies; it goes with understanding that children bring as much to school as they get from it; it goes with understanding the importance of firsthand experiences in and outside the classroom; it goes with an emphasis on the content of children's writing, rather than the mechanics of grammatical correctness; it goes with a deep, reasoned distrust of testing. Now that uniforms and setting are back, and time is short for firsthand experiences, and we test children and train them for tests until some of them are clinically depressed – now that we've got to this state of affairs, I wonder if, were it not for European legislation, smacking and caning in schools would come back too.

Here is some work from Set A in the Essex school:

Rules for Greeting a New Baby

1. Touch the baby's sweet soft hair. It's like soft ice cream straight from the ice cream van.
2. Kiss him on the head and feel his sweet soft skin.
3. Stroke his lovely skin. It's like a new leather sofa.
4. Feel his lovely tiny hands. They're just like cuddly toys.
5. Taste his sweet gentle kiss of his sweet skin.

6. Hear the baby cry, pick him up out of his cot, he will look at you and stop crying.
7. Look at his big bold eyes, they're as big as buses.
8. Buy him a rattle. Hear it shake like an old rusty car.

(Jake, 10)

Rules for Greeting a New Puppy

1. Go and buy some puppy food like porridge in a bowl.
2. Stroke his fur. It's like my Nan's knitting wool.
3. Feed him his food. He's like a pig eating greedily.
4. Hear him bark like my Dad when his team's just won a football match on t.v.
5. Tickle him under his tummy so he feels welcome.
6. Make him somewhere to sleep like my snugly bed.
7. Give him what he wants like a man on a street without a home at all.
8. Let him know he's cute like my mum does (not).
9. Clean him every day like my mum washes her clothes everyday.
10. And of course take care of him forever.

(Loren, 10)

Here is some work from the second, the Set B group:

Smell the baby like a brand new fragrance that people wear on their big night out.

Hold the baby's teddy. It's like the brand new teddy you had last Christmas.

Watch the baby crawl along the floor like a train on the tracks going to London.

Hear the baby bounce bounce bounce along the floor and cry cry cry again and again.

Feel the baby's hair. It feels like a brand new fairy coat.

Feel the baby's bottom. It feels like a silver dress.

(Robbie, 9)

... having a new pet is like a path waiting for you to run down ...

(Samantha, 9)

And here is some work from the Set C group:

A dog smells like flowers
a new dog sounds like ambulance sirens
a new dog smells like a fluffy pillow
a new dogs eyes are like sapphires
a new dogs paws are like babies feet

(James, 10)

James has simply not grasped the rules idea, but he probably would have done if he'd had the example of Set A children to listen to in my plenary session. Nevertheless, he has produced elementary similes. The next writer has produced one vivid image:

From 'Welcoming a New Bird'

Look at the lovely black spot on the end of its beak ...

There is a fashionable notion that boys need toughness in order to improve their reading and writing. I object to this because I have been taught over the years that we should not stereotype the sexes; that girls do not need books on ballet and horses, boys books on war and football. Here the boys back up my objections. 10-year-old Jake (a likely football lad, but you'll have to take my word for it) uses the word 'sweet' three times in his poem about a baby. Boys love babies as much as girls do.

WRITING BIOGRAPHY

Anthony Haynes, my editor, recommended that I read John Aubrey's *Brief Lives* (1690), which I had never even picked up before. However, after much study, I found nothing in the book that I could use with children between the ages of 7 and 14. But the notion of children writing biography stayed in my mind. I was reminded of a remark of Samuel Johnson's: 'There has rarely passed a life of which a judicious and faithful narrative would not be useful.' In one school I found some examples of lives that were still in their early stages, of which accounts had been written:

N___ G___ is 10 years old and has a brother called Z___ who is 7 years old. She lives with her mother D__ L___ S___ and dad S__ P__ G___ at _____ Her favourite subject is art and her least favourite subject is maths ... Her favourite season is autumn because she tries to catch all the leaves when they are falling from the trees ... Even though it is her favourite animal, she wouldn't like a crocodile for a pet because it's all scaly ... Her most embarrassing moment is when she was in playgroup and her brother started in the mornings and he was sick everywhere on purpose because he didn't want his mum to leave ... Her most annoying habit (her mum thinks) is that whenever she gets hold of a tomato sauce lid she clicks it up and down for hours on end.

(Emma, 10)

Frederick Arthur William Perkins [I can't resist printing all of this name, partly because I rarely meet Freds, and partly because his name is resonant of a certain kind of Englishness] has two sisters, Felice aged 14 and Daisy aged 12 ...

Frederick's favourite food is Chinese because his mum used to eat it every night before he was born ... Every time he has Chinese he has a cocktail and his favourite is chocolate ripple.

He has four chickens, two cats and two dogs. Their names are Titus, Flossy, Dougal, Splash, Mabel, Maisy, Betty and Dorse. I think they are funny names ...

He has always wanted to go to Spain because he gets to eat his favourite fruits which are plums because they are purple and juicy. His most embarrassing moment was when he fell down the stairs with no clothes on when someone was at the door. She said 'I can't look'.

Fred wants to be an astronaut ...

(Ashlea, 10)

Emma's best friend would laugh at her jokes, never break up with her, and be funny. Her perfect boyfriend would laugh a lot, be good looking and make her laugh!

(Anon., 10)

Because their teacher had suggested that the children should write their biographies of each other after conducting interviews, there is a freshness about this work. It also taught the children something about how to elicit relevant facts from another human being; how to takes notes quickly; and how to display their work. I felt that the wall that they had covered with the work was a useful PSME (Personal, Social and Moral Education) resource in the classroom. They referred to it often, and delighted in showing me things that had been written by them or about them. The work was pleasing because eccentricities emerged: the girl catching 'all the leaves when they are falling from the trees', and Frederick's favourite food: 'Chinese because his mum used to eat it every night before he was born.'

A way of writing that special case of biography, the auto kind, emerged later (see pp. 129–37, 'Confessions').

YOU SMOTE MY BACK: PUPIL TO TEACHER

In Michael Rosen's remarkable, dark anthology *The Penguin Book of Childhood* (1994), we hear many voices speaking eloquently across the centuries, from many different cultures, about what it is like to be a child, to teach one, to be a father or mother or grandfather to one, or even simply to be near one. Charles Lamb, writing a letter in the early nineteenth century (in Rosen, 1994, p. 77), destroys in the reader any delusions he or she might have had about the Romantics' feelings towards children: 'We have had a sick child, who, sleeping or not sleeping next to me, with a pasteboard partition between, killed my sleep. The little bastard is gone.'

Rosen's book suggests that, until very recently, violence, physical and verbal, was the accepted way of treating children. The cover painting sets the tone. Jan Steen's *The Village School* shows a schoolmaster hitting a crying child on the palm of his hand with a wooden spoon, probably designed for the purpose. Behind the desk, a girl winces at the imagined pain. From Ancient Greece, Protagoras (c.485–15BC) speaks for most adults quoted by Rosen when he writes about a boy, 'if he is willing, he obeys, but if not, then straighten him, just like a bent and twisted piece of wood, with threats and blows'. Samuel Smiles is told, when young, 'You will never be fit for anything but sweeping the streets of your native borough.' The later entries in the book do not allow us to feel smug about improvements in the treatment of children in our own time.

One of the most moving sentences comes from Ancient Egypt (New Kingdom) 2000–1500BC. A boy writes to his teacher, between three-and-a-half and four thousand years ago, this simple, telling sentence: 'I grew up beside you, you smote my back, and so your teaching entered my ear.'

At the end of a session in a school when I had been working on Thomas Hood's poem 'I Remember, I Remember' (in Sedgwick, 2000e), I read to the ninety-odd 9-, 10- and 11-year-olds in the school hall this sentence, and got them to say it after me. I mention the Hood to show that this was only a 'B' feature in a longer session: the children spent no more than twenty minutes following up the Egyptian boy's sentence, and this was after more than an hour writing poems about their memories (see Sedgwick, 1999a and 2000b for examples of this work).

I told the children that I felt moved to hear this ancient boy saying this sentence over the millennia. I pointed out how simple it was – just three statements, one the consequence of the other two – and said that he had inspired me to write some sentences addressed to two of my teachers at grammar school, back in the 1950s. I had written to my woodwork teacher:

Like the fool that I was when it came to practical things, I pinned my little ship to the bench with my brace and bit, and because I had made a hole in your workbench, you hit my palm with the steel ruler, and made me hate woodwork forever.

And then I wrote to my English teacher, remembering that my experience at grammar school wasn't all horrible:

You gave me a little book of poems from the school stock when I left, and it became the seed of my poetry library.

What would the children write to their teachers? I asked them to concentrate on positive things. This was because I wasn't very well known in the school, and I didn't want to embarrass the teachers, the children or myself. Rereading these sentences now, I am struck by how the clarity of the Egyptian boy's writing from the second millennium BC has influenced these writers in the third millennium AD:

You taught me that learning is everything when we are children,
and friends are not.

(Amy, 11)

What a questionable lesson that was!

You taught me to read loud, clear and frequent. I would not be
able to read now if it were not for you.

(Carmel, 10)

You taught me the life of art . . .

(Louise, 9)

You taught me how to walk through the Bible.

(John, 9)

You helped me through bad times, like when my mum and dad
split up. You were a good friend to me.

(Anon.)

What a compliment to a teacher this last piece is.

I flicked a bit of rubber across the room. You told me not to be
silly because it doesn't get you anywhere.

(Kit, 10)

The young teacher addressed here laughed: 'How often do we say
those things we swore we'd never say?'.

You taught me the violin. I still have the notes that we played
together.

(Samuel, 10)

You taught me about metaphor and similes. I still don't understand, only a bit.

(Jessie, 10)

You taught me courage and belief to make my own life up. You
changed my life. You gave me freedom.

(Luke, 9)

The piece that I liked best was this last one, because of two things: first, its awareness of how unfair the situation was that it describes and, second, because of its attempt to be fair to the teacher. This next is a child writing, unwittingly perhaps, about a moral problem:

> I wrote as fast as I could but I could not write fast but I suppose you weren't to know. You kept me in at lunchtime and it was unfair but you weren't to know.
>
> (Claire, 9)

I decided to do the same exercise in a school where I was well known and where the headteacher, a friend of mine of long standing, was leaving. There the sentences the children wrote had an extra poignancy:

> You helped me to know when to go on and when to go off.

> You showed me how to draw a realistic eye.

> You taught me how to eat a Brussels sprout.

> You held my hand when I had toothache.

> You lifted me up and spun me round on the playground.

> You said it was good to get muddy.

> You helped me when a scab fell off my knee.

> You told me what to do in school dinners when it was my first day.

> You helped me when my parents split up.

> You helped me when I fainted.

> You gave me courage before the play with a few words and ruffling my hair.

> You said the poem Full Fathom Five thy father lies of his bones are coral made those are pearls that were his eyes [whole poem had been learnt by heart and was written out, unpunctuated].

CONFESSIONS

'There Was a Peartree near Our Vineyard'

I claim this next lesson as unique. How many primary school children have been taught anything of the work of St Augustine (354–430)? This thinker, usually called Augustine of Hippo to distinguish him from the later Augustine of Canterbury, was a fourth-century Christian who wrote a book of his *Confessions* in which he told the story of his restless youth and his conversion from the heretical sect of Manicheans to Christianity. Because of his strong belief in the doctrine of original sin, he carried through his life a burden of guilt, about even the most trivial of his misdoings. We can see this in the passage quoted here. I think we can glimpse it in his remark: 'poetry is devil's wine', which I reckon Auden had in mind when he wrote, at the beginning of his *Collected Poems* (1976): 'Poetry is sin . . .'. Both remarks betray a distrust of the mantra magic side of poetry, the element of chant that takes it (thank God) beyond the commonsense. Elsewhere in Augustine's book, his guilt is about more serious sins than scrumping.

Augustine carried this burden in common with millions of Christians down the ages, including the comedian Billy Connolly, who memorably said that his Roman Catholic upbringing had left him with '"A" levels in Guilt', and with a character in Garrison Keillor's *Lake Wobegon Days* (1986), who articulated the predicament of the religious human being carrying more than his fair share of guilt, in a series of inspired and vivid footnotes. See pp. 251–74 of the paperback edition of this wonderful book, especially if you were brought up without the benefit of Guilt Education through one kind or another of fundamentalist religion.

I also carry this burden in common with St Augustine. Like many of our kind, I can feel guilty about things over which I have no control. I also feel guilty about times when I *do* have control over events, but when I have chosen for reasons of weakness (or original sin?) to do the wrong thing. Our kind's text is in St Paul's Letter to the Romans, 17:19: 'For the good that I would do I do not: but the evil that I would not, that I do' (echoed, eerily, in St Paul's near-contemporary, Ovid: '*Video meliora, proboque;/ Deteriora sequor*': 'I see the better way, and approve it; I follow the worse.'

One cold autumn day in 2000, without thinking about any of the dubious and troubling theology summarized so coarsely above, or about my dubious and coarse interpretation of that theology, I read to two classes – one composed of 7- and 9-year-olds, the other of 10- and 11-year-olds – some words by Saint Augustine. They are about the guilt that Augustine still felt in his old age about an incident he remembered from his childhood. Notice how clear this prose is. Notice, too, how little there is in it to baffle children:

> There was a pear-tree near our vineyard, loaded with fruit that was attractive neither to look at or to taste. Late one night a band of ruffians, myself included, went off to shake down the fruit and carry it away, for we had continued our games out of doors, as was our pernicious habit. We took away an enormous quantity of pears, not to eat them ourselves, but simply to throw them to the pigs. Perhaps we ate some of them, but our real pleasure consisted in doing something that was forbidden.
>
> (in Rosen, 1994, p. 11)

'Our real pleasure consisted in doing something that was forbidden.' That sentence means something to every human being who has grown into adulthood, whether guilt-stricken or not. Augustine has summed up something universal here, and the children in this remote Norfolk school recognized that. We all have an inbuilt need in us to rebel. I had to explain two words, of course – 'ruffian' and 'pernicious'. Then I confessed something of my own:

> When I was at grammar school in the 1950s, there was a geography teacher called Mr T——. He was a weak man, or that is how we saw him at the time, and that is how I recall him now. Flat strawy hair, the usual uniform of male teachers of this time: old tweed jacket with leather elbow patches, white shirt, modestly patterned and coloured tie, flannel trousers. The main point about him (at least for the purposes of this story) was that he 'couldn't keep control'. We gave him a bad time in his lessons. In Room A, next to the Assembly Hall, we used to shuffle our feet when he turned to the blackboard, and stop immediately when he turned round to face us. One boy, Alan Styles, who had a gift for satire and mimicry, once asked Mr T—— a basic question about the course, and when the teacher answered it, Styles stood up, leaned on his desk, and said, smirking in the manner of a television quiz show host of the times (Michael Miles, I believe he was called) 'Henry T——, you are right.' Once we put Swan Vestas matches down Mr T——'s chalk, having bored though the

chalk first with compass points, in the false hope that the chalk would ignite as he wrote on the board.

I hope that healing happened here, for me, not for poor Mr T., as I made my confession to the children. I invited them to write their own confessions. This section, then, is composed of children writing about naughty things that they have done in the past, that they can't forget. Here are three from the younger children:

It all started when my guinea pigs had just had babies. I really wanted to see them. My mum said I couldn't because they were too young to be picked up and because their mum would get nervous. So when my mum was doing the ironing and my dad was out at his friends and my brother was out playing with his friend I sneaked outside into the garage and opened the door and carefully picked one up. 'Ahhh' I cried, it was so sweet and so cuddly. I was just about to put it back when suddenly Ashley barged in and said gimme that pig I want to hold it. He snatched it off me and said ughhh and dropped it. But it lived except it had a bad limp. After he dropped it he ran to tell mum that I dropped a pig so I was grounded for three days.

(Amy, 8)

I note here the use of a second 'because' to introduce a second subordinate clause. There is a very mature use of this word later on in Melissa's writing, as well. I have become convinced over recent years that children often have a subtler grasp of the grammatical and syntactical nuances of language than we appreciate, and that the fact that they cannot define a subordinate clause (for example) is beside the point. They can use one.

One day when I was in the forest there was a toadstool and my mum said don't kick it and then I kicked it and my mum shouted at me and my dad threw a fir cone at me.

(Timmy, 7)

When my mum picked me up from school I wanted to go round Amy's and my mum said no so I dropped my lunchbox and kicked it across the playground. I got wrong off my mum for showing her up and she told dad when he got home and he gave me a great big wallop.

I got sent to my room and I got no pocket money for four

> weeks. When I got to my room I got a piece of paper and wrote I was going to run away and because I had loads of bags in my room I got some clothes out and put them in a bag. I got a stick and put the bag on the stick and then I went out the back door and told my mum and dad I was going to run away to Newark where my Grandad lives. I didn't run away, I hid in the garden. My brother found me and told my mum and dad.
>
> (Melissa, 8)

Here are some examples from the older children:

> I was out in my garden sitting staring up into the sky, bored. I couldn't think of what to do. An idea struck me. There in the middle of the garden was a swing ball. I started hitting the ball first one way and then the other. Unfortunately my sister came out and said 'Can I play?' But I said 'No, I like playing on my own' but she didn't take any notice of me. She said something like 'You can't stop me'. That made me angry, very angry. I was playing happily until she came out. I told her she could play after me. She was being really horrible so I lost my temper and threw the bat. By accident it hit her in the hand and I broke her finger so she had to go to hospital. And I got told off. My mum said the police might come, just to warn me. I cried.
>
> (Victoria, 10)

> It was a cold rainy day and I was stuck indoors. My mum was doing a jigsaw puzzle with me. I had a piece of the jigsaw puzzle but I couldn't see where it fitted. I started to get angry. I screamed and hit my mum. The jigsaw puzzle went flying as I flung it across the table. I knocked a glass out of the cupboard on purpose and it smashed. I ran around until I was worn out. I got on the sofa and fell asleep to my Mum's joy. When I woke I was the most innocent three-year-old in the whole world.
>
> (Prudence, 10)

This account, obviously, derives from tellings of the story by Prudence's parents. I can almost hear the parental expressions of joy, the later description of the 'the most innocent three-year-old in the world'. None of this detracts from the writer's account. I have written earlier about the power of the story. Here a family story serves like the stories of a race – the Bible, or the Koran, or the

Scandinavian myths – to give meaning to relationships and biography, and to make those relationships more secure:

> When I was ten it was summer and there were lots of baby ducklings and I saw one on the road. I asked mum if I could keep it. My dad shouted 'No!'. So I screamed 'Was I talking to you?' and my mum said 'If you ever speak like that to your dad again'. I ran out and got hold of the duck and ran to the back door. My mum was standing there. Tears were running down my face. My mum felt sorry for me so she asked to look at it. She got a box and said 'Take it up to your bedroom'. I did and gave it some rice Krispies mixed up with water and I gave it a separate bowl of milk mixed with water. I stayed up all night and the next day it was still alive. So I went downstairs and outside in the shed because we used to keep fish and I knew we had a fishtank which was quite big. I found it and put some kitchen roll, newspaper, cotton wool, and got some food for it. I cared for it for about two months. I let it swim in my pond and I let it run around after flies but as it got older it got weaker and Alice's friend slept over that night and we all cried for days. It's now buried in my garden with a wooden gravestone and a flower on the top. My dad still tells me that I should have left it on the road. My mum says it was probably ill and that's why its mum left it on the road.
>
> (Victoria, 10)

> At our old house in Maidstone in Kent when I was four or five years old I waited for my mum to watch t.v., for my dad to go out. Then I went downstairs and opened a cupboard, opened a packet of M&Ms. My dog came over and started to get friendly with me. Me and my dog shared them but then we had about five M&Ms left. To my horror mum came in the kitchen and saw me so I got wrong but my dog comforted me and what was so unfair mum ate the last of the M&Ms.
>
> (Sophie, 9)

How badly the parents come out of all this! 'I got wrong off my mum for showing her up and she told dad when he got home and he gave me a great big wallop.' They seem to bear grudges, and to be unnecessarily violent, and vindictive mentally, too: 'My mum said the police might come, just to warn me.' ('Got wrong', I should explain, is local dialect (mid-Norfolk) for 'got into trouble'.)

In another school, a teacher, Sally Wilson, contributed her confession. Many teachers seem unaware of the usefulness of writing alongside the children: it teaches the children that writing is not merely something that they have to do because they are told to do it but, much more significantly, that it is something that we can all do to keep ahead in the life-long project of trying to understand our human predicament. As Miss Wilson bent over her notebook in the silent classroom, they were being helped to understand that writing is something that we all do in order to make sense of our past, present and future:

A long time ago when I was 9 I thought I was very grown up.

There was a small boy at my school called Max who had blue eyes and blond curls.

Max followed me around the playground everywhere, desperate to play with me.

Of course, I didn't care. I was far too grown up to play with little children.

One cold September morning when I was feeling particularly grown up, was I terribly horrible to poor little Max.

I explained to him that he was far too small and unimportant to even speak to me.

Max's eyes welled up with huge fat tears which cascaded down his cheeks.

I pretended to be tough and not care, but really deep inside I felt awful.

Nobody knew that I had been mean that day except Max and myself.

I didn't tell anyone but I felt sick with guilt for weeks afterwards. I made sure I always played with everyone from that day on.

(Sally Wilson)

In Sally Wilson's class, children wrote:

> When I was younger, but not much younger, my mum had a hideous dress. It was covered with revolting pink and yellow flowers. Well I couldn't put up with the embarrassment, so I hid it in the least obvious place (the shed) in a bucket. But what I didn't know was that the bucket was full of soil and water. My mum was horrified and she cut my pocket money for 2 months.
>
> (Sarah, 9)

> When I was 3 I did something naughty.
>
> I crept up the stairs guiltily to the bathroom and locked the door.
>
> What made it worse was my mum was in the bath singing [indecipherable title] by Rod Stewart. I took the key out of the hole and crept down the stairs. I went into the garden and got my bright yellow spade, dug up my mum's bright roses and put the key in the hole, and covered it up. I knew my dad knew because everyone in the house was shouting my name. I ran into the house and he made me tell where it was but by that time I couldn't remember.
>
> (Tilda, 9)

When Tilda originally told this story to the class, it went something like this:

> I locked my mum in the bathroom once when she was having a bath. I buried the key in the garden.

The rest of the account emerged under requests like 'Can you tell us what happened before you did the naughty thing?' and questioning: 'Where did you put the key? How did the rest of the family find out?' and so on. It is interesting that these questions have not only elicited the details that they ask for, but have also elicited other details that I didn't request, or expect: mum singing a Rod Stewart song, for example, and the 'bright yellow' spade.

Later, in a secondary school, I read to Year 8 a poem based on my experience at grammar school:

John Crystal

John Crystal was the kindest teacher
　　I ever had:
More generous than rain on grass
　　But many times as sad.

For Johnny Crystal, he could not
　　Control his fountain pen
Let alone the boys then changing
　　Into gentlemen.

There were a hundred ways that we
　　Eclipsed John Crystal's sun:
'What did you do in school today?'
　　'We had a bit of fun.'

Then one Monday night I walked
　　Back for something I'd
Forgotten in the mayhem of
　　Skinning Crystal's hide.

Past the headmaster's office and
　　Through empty rooms I move.
They're quiet as the time before
　　Needle touches groove.

Then, piano, comes the sound
　　Of the gentlest of sort of jazz
From one of the treasured records that,
　　I'm sure my father has.

I nudge the hall door open.
　　His gown slung on a chair,
His head asway to silent drums,
　　John Crystal's playing there.

His eyes are closed. His tie is loose.
　　On the piano stand
His coffee mug and ashtray
　　At the beck of his hand.

Now, John Crystal, when I hear
　　Brubeck and Desmond play
I think of how we tortured you
　　Day after cruel day.

I think of all the times the sun
   Went dim across your world
because of the gentleman wit
   We nobly hurled.

I see your full head swaying
   And your discarded gown
And hear the fractured melody
   Even I couldn't drown.

The secondary pupils listened to the Augustine, and to this poem, and then came up with several terrifying confessions. One involved giving a toddler brother aspirins, having told him that they were sweets: the child had to go to hospital and have his stomach pumped. Another girl, aware that her little sister was frightened of ants, shut her in the garage where there was an ants' nest.

With these confessions, we are in the world of healing. Facing up to what we regret having done involves implicitly asking for forgiveness, and that is a healing process.

The chapter has not been as fragmentary as I had anticipated. Maybe I am more sure of things than I thought. Maybe my instinct for order is too certain. I also feel that I have not fulfilled certain tentative promises made at the beginning of the chapter about healing.

More fragments now, as I quote children writing about travel.

5

A part of experience,
a part of school

Travel, in the younger sort, is a part of education; in the elder, a part of experience. He that travelleth into a country before he hath some entrance into the language, goeth to school, not to travel. (Francis Bacon)

INTRODUCTION

This chapter picks up the theme of Chapter 4. I am, again, concerned here with the kind of prose that we, rightly or wrongly, deem to be lower in status than that of the great novelists, like Jane Austen and Charles Dickens. And yet, in this chapter, I am not so much concerned with the utterly trivial – advertisements and lists and the rest – but with what seems to us (at least when we write it, those of us who do) to be very important: our travel notes.

And nearly all of us write these. I know this, because I have been saving postcards from friends for the past twenty years. These quotations are from my friend John Cotton, and they all come from France. I am only quoting these (he trots all over the globe) just to narrow the choice down a fraction. I could have quoted other friends, and a hundred other places: Pontins at Great Yarmouth, Pompeii, Sydney, London . . .

Sitting on my own, before me a splendid view of hills, fields and woods, reading a Rose Macaulay I found in the lavatory of La Tour!

Went to Lascaux yesterday. Remarkable. It is one long panorama stretching the length of the cave – horses, bison, reindeer in a great sweep of movement. In spite of the theories of ritual and magic, what comes over is the sheer joy of artistic expression!

Made our pilgrimage to the confluence of the rivers Dordogne and Vezere today and ate galettes and drank cider there, as ever. Misty rainy morning, brilliant afternoons.

Heaven knows where we are except it is very beautiful! The nearest shop is several miles away in a place called Cubas (pronounced 'cuba', – a little disorientating!

Everyone who can write a postcard can write travel at some level or another. If you don't believe me, look over the cards you have kept and, even more important, look at what you write from your next holiday. Make postcard poems of them. This little piece was developed from a note written on holiday as the writer watched young people clowning in the hotel pool:

A young man makes a base
of a swaying totem pole
in the bright blue pool.
A woman screams on his shoulders
and higher still
another woman screams on hers.
It can't last much.

(Jack, 13)

You can give the poems a kind of structure by making them haiku or tanka or cinquains.

If you can get the word 'like' into your little postcard poem, in its simile usage, that will help:

Man in the Pool

He says
he is old now.
Round pink shoulders, water
lifts and falls, like blue and silver
mountains.

(Jack, 13)

But perhaps we are thinking of something less ephemeral than a card . . .

Some fifteen years ago, I was lucky enough to gain a place on a course for jaded headteachers, who had done ten years or more. It wasn't advertised like that. It was an OTTO (one term training opportunity) course in management. By the nature of the course, almost all were men – just two women – who had been headteachers in the wake of Plowden education, and who had then suffered the slings and arrows of the monetarist revolution. We were having to get clued up on alien notions (alien, at any rate, to me) like 'cost-effectiveness', 'managing personnel resources' and 'privatization of groundstaff'. We had to attend a local university for a whole autumn term, and discuss the running of schools and the like: decision-making styles, participatory management, getting the best from people-resources.

My luck was in having the term away from school, not in gaining management training. My lack of interest in the managerialism that had become the indispensable condition of headship was becoming obvious to others (who didn't see my failure in the same light: I was slightly proud of it, on the quiet). During a preparatory meeting the previous July, we were instructed not to go into our schools at all because, apart from it being a learning time for us, the term would also be a learning time for our deputies. It would be practice for them in the business of headship to which, in due time, they would presumably be expected to climb, and to shine, by demonstrating an understanding that, among other things, a school's personnel was its greatest resource, that its image was everything and that if you replaced paper towels with hand blowers, you could save £145.60 per year.

There was a period of three weeks between the beginning of the school term and the beginning of the university term. Three free weeks! The thought bowled me over. We were supposed to sit at home and study in preparation for the course. I took the tutors at the university at their word, and made myself totally absent from school. But I went with my wife and son (he was then 7 years old) to Malta, taking with me, of course, all my management books.

None of us had been to the little island before. We saw churches, especially St John's Co-cathedral, where there is a Caravaggio painting of 'The Beheading of St John'. The three of us marvelled over it, horrified. We lay about on beaches. I remember the brightly striped boats rocking gently in the exotically named Marsamxett harbour, and the pizza restaurants in Republic Square in Valetta. I remember the weak, cheap, delightful local wine, and a beer called 'Hopleaf'. My son remembers firecrackers being set off deafeningly on various beaches to celebrate the victory of one political party or another in elections.

We travelled both the main island and Gozo, its little sister, on the old buses and watched football at the Taq Qali stadium. We walked around the third island, Comino, deserted except for some millionaire's mansion down by the beach, and bathed in the blue sea (for once the cliché was apt). One day we saw dolphins following our boat, and we stood up in awe at the sight, and at our luck.

Later, back in England, a headteacher of a local school complained in a letter to a newspaper:

> How can parents expect us to deliver the National Curriculum when they take their children out of school during the school terms?

I couldn't believe the arrogance of this. I felt sure that my son had been learning more in Malta than he would have been learning, sitting at his desk in school. I thought of him, looking at the Caravaggio, and reflected that he had learned more in that five minutes than he would have learned in a week with the fledgling National Curriculum, with its handcuffs marked 'levels'. I agree with Bacon, quoted above, that for the young travel is a school. In addition, though, I think that travel is also a school for the rest of us. Who would not be a more educated human being through having been to a foreign country, and seen its culture, both in the high art sense of the world, and in the sociological sense, the way ordinary lives are lived, the pavements, the buses, the bars?

A large part of the travel school can be the writing we do when we are travelling, and when we get back home. Now travel writing is, I am told, a problem for editors of magazines and newspapers, especially in late August and September every year. This is because holiday-makers have a great time somewhere – in France or Frinton, in Indianapolis or in India, in Canada or the Canary Islands – and think that they can give readers a diluted version of that fine time by writing about it and getting an editor to publish what they have written, possibly with the snaps they have taken by the pool, or in the mountains, or in the Roman amphitheatre. But something significant is required to place the writer's name at the top of a page, and to earn a hundred pounds or so, and, more importantly, to transform the writer's good time into the reader's. The would-be travel writers miss out the yeast, and the editors' problem is that the articles that they receive are unpublishable. Perhaps Malcolm Muggeridge was right when he wrote in the *Observer* (5 September 1976): 'travelling [is], like war and fornication, exciting but not interesting'.

These travel accounts are perfect as records to go along with the writers' photographs, but no more. Paste them in the photograph albums! I know about this problem from the wrong end: I have written several joyous accounts of holidays, full of food, wine, Roman ruins, streets I've wandered up and down for hours, lizards on rocks, snakes in the road, and dolphins leaping from the Mediterranean. But I have not worked on them sufficiently to make them public. I suspect now that the editors were right to reject them. An editor told me that one mistake we failed travel writers make is to tell the story chronologically, when we should start with the most interesting part. We begin with picking up the hired Fiat at the airport, trundling our cases through Gatwick, or worse, locking our front door in Swindon or wherever. We should start with the disaster when our children fell into Etna, or the bullfight that exhilarated or horrified us, or the moment when we were really happy at a dinner table on a terrace – in all cases making sure our prose is vivid and gets across the facts and emotions.

A VICTORIAN ON HIS TRAVELS

What is good travel writing? Perhaps what these articles miss out can be seen in what is included in this late Victorian extract. This passage comes from *An Account of Palmyra and Zenobia with Travels and Adventures in Bashan and the Desert* by Dr William Wright, first published in 1895 (1987):

> In descending the mountain from the baths we started [startled] several very small whitish hares, and saw many holes of foxes and jackals. The ground was strewed with rock crystals, which glanced like diamonds in the sunlight. A low range of hills screened Karyetein from our view, but we had steered our course by a peak which we knew was in line with the village. In the bright atmosphere the distance seemed as nothing, yet it was a most weary ride across a level plain, which was all seamed with

footpaths, some of which had been trod by Abraham and his emigrants.

We passed several abandoned Bedawi encampments, but we saw no living thing in a ride of over three hours, except a few hares and bustards, and an occasional eagle hastening overhead to its prey. On reaching Karyetein, however, we learned that we must have passed under the very noses of the plundering Beda-win, who were hovering about our path in the mountains.

What is the yeast here? What makes this good travel writing? First, the simplicity of the style: there is nothing fancy in these para-graphs (which are typical of the whole book); any flourishes are discarded in the interest of a need to convey what the experience was like. There is stability in the style: shortish sentences, a lack of showing off. There is no unnecessary use of the passive mode. Second, that simile: the rocks 'glancing like diamonds'; it sparkles itself, like a diamond, partly because it is on its own. Note, too, that the brightness is picked up again later in the passage (the 'bright atmosphere'). There is a historical context: Wright finds significance in his experience by knowing about Abraham and his 'emigrants'. The passage has a dramatic ending: what might have happened. I must face up to the fact that good travel writing always has an element of adventure in it, and is therefore difficult to do in the context of the package holiday, where we value safety above the surprise element.

Here is some more travel writing, about an event that was as dangerous as any traveller might want:

> the cloud shot up like the trunk of a pine tree ... Sometimes it was white, sometimes darker ... There was earth and cinders in the cloud ... The cinders fell into the ships with pieces of burning rock ... There were huge flames everywhere ... People did not know whether to trust in the safety of their houses, or to run to the open fields, where the hot ash continued to fall.

That is Pliny the Younger's account of his father watching the destruction of Pompeii (in Santini, 1991). It was the older man's last piece of research because he, too, became a victim of the catastrophe.

I always keep a journal when I am on holiday. I have taken to heart Samuel Johnson's resonant advice to James Boswell:

> He advised me to keep a journal ... fair and undisguised. He
> said it would be a very good exercise ... I told Johnson that I put
> down all sorts of little incidents in it. 'Sir', said he, 'there is
> nothing so little for so little a creature as man. It is by studying
> little things that we attain the great knowledge of having as little
> misery and as much happiness as possible.'
>
> (Boswell, [1791] 1906)

My Spanish journal for August 2000 is in front of me as I type. I
try not to travel without my journal: as Oscar Wilde's Gwendolyn
said (about her diary), one should always have something sensa-
tional to read on the train. I do not know now whether it has the
qualities of Wright's prose, or whether it is the kind of showy
material that thousands of travel writers manqué hopefully send in
every autumn. However, it is evidence of me 'studying little
things':

> I am sitting at a table on the terrace, the sound of Spanish voices
> around me, the shadows of the willow leaves waving across the
> white cloth. I have a glass of house white and am waiting for a
> Spanish omelette, chips and salad. I feel suddenly relaxed and
> liberated: liberated from work, both in schools and from the
> study. The proofs.
>
> The incessant water sounds. The Spanish of families and
> staff ...
>
> I have a little desk to write at. I can see the balcony and other
> rooms, white like Caerphilly cheese. I can see palm trees, the
> rough striated bark like something on a pineapple, the long
> leaves covering the top like an Afro haircut or one of those dogs
> you think can't see anything. Purple flowers climb a balcony. I
> can hear the constant sound of breeze through trees ...
>
> On the road to Ronda, we meet about two hundred goats, led
> by the bell goat, and pushed on by the leathery-faced goatherd.
> How quiet they are says Daniel. Indeed, all you can hear is the
> gentle trotting. And how clean they look. I lean out of the
> window and take a photograph ...
>
> In the gutter in Calle de Seville in Ronda at midday, outside
> Bar Jose Mari. What in Ireland would be called a jaunting car
> tinkles and trots up the road ...
>
> Midday. The white square at Montehaque. They are preparing
> for the feria. In this bar (one of at least four) a Rangers pennant
> hangs on the wall among the Blessed Virgins and the pop stars.

In the church, a loud woman displays lilies, like a Matron in an English country church. A Downs boy, in immaculate long fawn shorts and white T-shirt, jumps over the cables littering the square. Wanders towards the church. Pretty olive-skinned girls are everywhere. Above the white two-storey buildings, the rocks that have been there for almost all time. I am the invisible watcher as the bell strikes Midday. Time for a Cruzcampo . . .

By the poolside. The water like chainmail, bright, glassy, beautiful chainmail. Two boys at the other end look like something out of a Hockney painting.

DRAFTING

Drafting is, rightly, heavily emphasized in the National Curriculum (English Key Stages 1–4, p. 21). I always tell children how much drafting and redrafting my own work required. I left my notebook untouched for a while when I got home, playing around with my photographs and talking with my son about our holiday. It occurred to me for the first time how holiday snaps could be of great value in this kind of work. I then redrafted the passage. (For my notes on drafting, see Sedgwick, 1997.) Almost all writers draft and redraft: few produce acceptable, let alone good, prose at the first sitting. Rudyard Kipling (a writer whose views we can forgive because he wrote so well) talks about letting a story 'drain' after a first draft, and then reworking it, and finding out that much of what he wrote is unnecessary. I often find after this draining period that I need to add material.

Children need to be introduced to this method of working. Browne (whose 1993 book on children and writing contains more sense than many others) says:

> The process of drafting encourages children to shape and reshape their ideas on paper, on the computer or on tape before producing the final version of their writing.

I would go further than Browne here, and suggest that there is no 'final version'. 'A poem', as Valery tells (Auden 1971), 'is never finished, only abandoned.' Concentration on what is finished, what is presentable, what is good to look at for parents, inspectors and so on is not necessarily educational. We should concentrate instead on the process rather than on the product. What (in other words) are we learning as we write? This is a more interesting, a more educational question than 'What have we learnt, now that this is displayed or published'? All modern emphasis on league tables and SATs results is evidence of an inability to understand that education is always what *is* happening, not what *has* happened. This book is evidence of my learning, or a glimpse of its process, not a record of it. Writers know that they change as they write, that they write in obedience to an impulse to teach themselves.

Here is my new draft, as abandoned. If you don't like it, it doesn't matter because, if one writes about somewhere, one knows it better, and I know my part of Spain better because of the making of these notes:

A table on the terrace. The sound of Spanish voices around me, talking of who knows what. The shadows of the willow leaves wave across the perfect white tablecloth. I have a glass of house white wine – Merceres, it is called – and am waiting for a Spanish omelette, chips and salad.

A Spanish omelette isn't like the ones I make at home. The main thing is potato: Diego tells me that you fry it in slices, gently, making sure it doesn't go brown. Then you stir in the forked egg. It can be served cold. The locals use it for picnics.

I feel suddenly relaxed and liberated: liberated from work, both in schools and from the study. The proofs I've spent a week on feel a long time ago now. And now they're a long distance away.

The incessant water sounds. The Spanish of families and staff . . . The omelette comes. It is cold, and delicious.

In our room, I have a little desk to write at. I can see the balcony and other rooms, balconies and walls, all white like Cheshire cheese. I can see palm trees, the rough scored bark like something on a pineapple, the long leaves covering the top like an Afro haircut or one of those dogs you think can't see anything. Purple flowers climb a balcony. I can hear the constant sound of breeze through trees, and the water trickling in the little river that dries up in some summers.

On the road to Ronda, we meet about two hundred goats, led by the bell goat, and pushed on by the leathery-faced goatherd. How quiet they are, says Daniel. Indeed, all you can hear is the gentle trotting. And how clean they look. I lean out of the window and take a photograph.

Later . . . I'm in the gutter in Calle de Seville in Ronda at midday, outside Bar Jose Mari. But gutters in Spain are the places

where the best cafe tables are, and they are the perfect places to drink little bitter coffees. What in Ireland would be called a jaunting car tinkles and trots up the road ... A Sheffield United Supporter, in his red and white stripes, sits with his family at the next table. Spanish people queue at the church on the other side of the square for Mass. It is the feast of the Assumption.

Down the road is the taja, or gorge. The town is simply split in two by this great crack in the world. You look down over a hundred metres, and see the backs of birds flying. Once a Spaniard told me here, as we looked down into the gorge, that they threw men over the walls during the Civil War. Which side threw which? I asked. Both, he replied.

All around Ronda, there are men growing old in this town. You see them, small of stature in the streets, smoking, in their open-necked shirts and slacks, talking to each other in groups. Wherever you see them, you have to reflect on a terrible fact: some of them fought for Franco's fascists, some for the Republicans, the loyalists. Now they chat amicably in the street ...

Midday. This is the white square at the little village of Montehaque, a few hundred metres up the mountain from Molino ... They are preparing for the feria, the feast of their village patron saint. In this bar (one of at least four) a Rangers pennant hangs on the wall among the Blessed Virgins and the pop stars: an

improbable place for the most Protestant football club in Europe, or the world. I like to think that perhaps these people are ignorant of the religious tensions in Ulster and Glasgow. In the church, a loud woman arranges lilies, and steps back to judge the effect of her work, in one way like a Matron in an English country church, in other ways nothing like her. A Downs boy, in immaculate long fawn shorts and white T-shirt, jumps carefully over the cables littering the square. He wanders towards the church. Pretty olive-skinned girls are everywhere. Above the white two-storey buildings, the rocks that have been there for almost all time are still there. I am the invisible watcher as the bell strikes midday. Time for a Cruzcampo . . .

By the poolside. The water is like glassy chainmail. Two boys at the other end look like boys in a Hockney painting.

Later, I found an old notebook with writing in it about a holiday at the same place five years before, and a sketch that my wife had made while we waited to go into the Pileta caves.

To the caves at Pileta. They're surrounded by rocks like Auden's forehead. Drawings 20,000 years old. A pregnant horse, diagrammatic men, bisons, bulls, notches for counting. Led around by a charming Spaniard in a group of Germans, British, Spanish,

Swiss, and he spoke to us all in our own language. The stalactites and stalagmites grow at a rate of 1 centimetre per century.

I read Wright's and my own passage to some children early in September. There is not enough children's writing in this chapter because you have to catch it early in the school year. By the time September is over, the children's memories of their activities in the summer have faded enough to take the bloom off any notes that they might make. This writing idea has lost its power, and I must wait until next September before I can try it again.

I told the children – and this is very important – that travel writing can be about places just down the road, the local park, for example, or the local swimming pool, as well as time spent in Spain or Africa. It can be about 'days out' as well as weeks away in Scotland or America. It is all too easy to make less-well-off children feel inferior. I dread the unwitting snobbery of those maps of the world that appear in some classroom walls in September, with everybody's holiday destination marked with strings attached to children's names. We learn from these that Richard went to Los Angeles, Kelly to Torremolinos, and John, Bethany and Freddie to Clacton, Hastings or Ramsgate. As I child, I remember the habitual answer to 'Where did you go for your holidays?' and my reply, 'We had days out', meaning trips down the Thames.

I suggested two techniques to the children. The first was the use of the present tense (see Chapter 1): this can provide an immediacy that the past does not. It can make the reader feel that he or she is there. The second technique is to be conscious as you write of what the five senses can do for your writing, much as they can do a great deal for your perception:

I can hear children shouting outside my brother's house on Guernsey. Inside it is silent. Suddenly rap music blasts and pounds through the speakers. Mike, my brother, asks me if I want a drink of Red Bull. I thank him. It was like cherryade fizzed up. The room smelt like smoke. I sat on a chair. It was as soft as clouds. Chris came in and turned the t.v on to The Box, which is a music station . . . We went outside to have our picture taken. The sun sparkled on the double glazing. It was an extra-ordinary day.

(Matthew, 10)

I am sitting in the sand with the sun shining in my eyes. People talk and play in the sea. The sand is gritty between my toes. Seagulls squawk. It hurts my ears. A small brown dog is barking, chasing its tail. I cannot feel my legs now. Sand feels heavy on my legs. Sand runs through my fingers. The wind is now coming across my face. The clouds now hide the sun. I am trying to get out of the sand. It's hard. I pull and pull. I cannot move. I am calling my brother. He is pulling me out of the sand. My sister is laughing out loud. I get out. I am chasing my sister. I am getting near the sea. Me and my sister have landed in our sandcastle. We are laughing.

(Sarah, 10)

Originally, this piece had present participle verbs where it now has main verbs. In other words, where we now read 'talk and play', the writer had written 'talking and playing'. Children use present participles readily. I suspect. This piece also has Suffolk speech in it: 'The wind is now coming across my face. The clouds now hide the sun.' That use of 'now' . . .

The Dome

We have just sat down in the food court at the Millennium Dome. I've been on two rides, Timekeepers and the Body. If I had to choose which was best, I would have to choose the Body. Recently our Dutch friends have come over. They came with us. Their little boy and my little brother shot up like fireworks when they heard the heart. They were so frightened. The brain talked like a human being.

The journey was long and boring because I was sitting by my own. I survived on Coke and peanuts. I must have had at least four cans of Coke and two packets of peanuts. When we got there, all I wanted to do was sit down and go to sleep.

Well, I have to go for now. I'll speak to you after this ride, which is called Our World. Bye!

(Anon., 10)

Anon. only wrote the paragraph beginning 'The journey was long and boring' because I had insisted. He thought that he had finished, hence his word 'Bye!' This was the equivalent of younger children writing in their stories 'Then they had their tea and went to bed.'

Here are some more examples of children's travel writing:

I am sitting in my bed listening to the cleaners outside. They are blowing the leaves away. I am sitting up right now, now listening. My brother in the next bed is awoken by the commotion. He is sitting up as well. We clamber out of bed still half asleep, plodding sleepily to the wardrobe, yanking it open, and reaching for our swimming costumes . . .

I breathe in fresh air. I pull the inflatable whale towards me and place it in the water. The sun shines brightly on the water, making it shimmer. I heave myself on to the whale and lean on it dreamily and flow wherever over the water. Suddenly I feel myself tip and SPLASH! My brother had tipped me up and I am trying to drown him.

(Anon., 11)

Mallorca

I am travelling across Bellevue Lake and I can hear the jetskis in the background. I pass the island and I can feel the smoke from the barbecues. We are now approaching the coral reef and I can see the coloured fish . . .

I can see a man selling fruit and he is shouting 'Melonmelonie' so I go to buy a pineapple and a melon.

I have finished the fruit and I am heading back to the hotel.

(Justin, 10)

We went to Egypt. Near the pyramids I saw an old lady whose eyes were completely white. She had cataracts, and nobody had any money to make them better. I saw a shop called Hapi Papyrus. I saw a Nefertiti Pharmacy . . . The pyramids were wonderful. We went to a mosque. It was all patterns. We smelt sandalwood. We went to a Coptic church, and the guide called us the sunshine family. Some children said to me Hello hello money and held out their hands.

(James, 9)

Sophie Chipperfield, in her school in Essex, read the Wright passage and mine to her children:

I can remember floating on top of the waves where my step-dad used to work in Spain, Calalavada. My hotel was called San Eloy. I can remember a man called Jamie shouting on his megaphone every morning at six o'clock 'Good Morning San Eloy' . . . I had squid in batter with spaghetti hoops . . .

. . . Lots of the baboons came on our car and one was on the driver's side wing mirrors, one went to the toilet down the side. It was really funny. We could tell which animals liked the sun and which liked the rain. A baboon left an apple on the bonnet of our car. We went on and the apple was still there. The biggest went to the driver's side and then it went for the apple. We thought that it was going to hit the car but all it wanted was the apple.

I can remember going down a slide which was as steep as a mountain but when I was going down all you could see was white splashes which was the water.

(Anon., 10)

Byron wrote a poem about leaving Malta (in Crossley-Holland, 1986). It isn't a great poem, but its clever rhyming and its worldly bluntness make it typical of him. I told the children in one class that he obviously hadn't liked his stay there much. I explained some terms: La Valette is a reference to the capital city, Valetta; sirocco is the Sahara wind when he reaches that part of the Mediterranean; packets are boats arriving in the harbour – apparently without the anticipated letters for Byron; his Excellency is, presumably, the ambassador. I talked about the rhyme – especially 'yawn, Sirs/ dancers' – and suggested that the children did not try to ape this style.

Adieu, ye joys of La Valette!
Adieu, sirocco, sun and sweat!
Adieu, thou palace rarely entered!
Adieu, ye mansions where I've – ventured!
Adieu, ye cursed street of stairs!
(How surely he who mounts you swears!)
Adieu, ye merchants often failing!
Adieu, thou mob forever failing!
Adieu, ye packets, without letters!
Adieu, ye fools – who ape your betters! . . .
Adieu, that stage that made us yawn, Sirs,
Adieu, his Excellency's dancers!

Had the children had a holiday or a day out when everything seemed to go wrong?

Goodbye the Mumbles where it rained every day except the first
   Sunday.
Goodbye the Mumbles where the Dylan Thomas pub was
   closed.
Goodbye the Mumbles where we got soaked in the High Street
   looking for new anoraks.
Goodbye the Mumbles Castle where I slipped in the mud and
   got soaked.

(Jim, 10)

My mum and dad saw the paintings
My mum and dad saw the Globe
But the London Eye was too crowded, and I couldn't go on it.

That piece of writing seemed to have more mileage in it, so I
suggested that the writer should think of other London successes
for her parents, and repeat the line about her London Eye
disappointment:

My mum and dad took us down the Thames. I liked it.
My mum and dad went on a bus without a roof
But the London Eye was too crowded, and I couldn't go on it.

My mum and dad had a pizza and so did I.
My mum and dad saw the pigeons in Trafalgar Square
But the London Eye was too crowded, and I couldn't go on it.

We saw the guards at Buckingham Palace
and we saw the Houses of Parliament
But the London Eye was too crowded, and I couldn't go on it.

(Sarah, 8)

'Travel, in the younger sort, is a part of education' wrote Francis
Bacon. We do not take the fun away from holidays by seeing them
as times for learning: on the contrary, we put more fun into them,
because to learn is to engage with life. We make life more explicitly
sensual by understanding what we are doing, and why we are
doing it. Entertainment, on the other hand, that appears to be about
fun, to be about the sensations, is both deeply superficial and
deeply puritanical because it ignores what we are. It pretends. It is
wholly about the guinea. So is the official: that too pretends to be
concerned with what we are as human beings. But instead it is
concerned with the surface, the guinea.

We are human beings trying to understand how to live in a world that is disturbingly and excitingly varied. We are human beings that by our nature see the sun and see, at the same time, not an official guinea, not a guinea that rewards superficial success in some league table, but the Heavenly Host singing 'Holy, Holy, Holy'.

In any event, we turn now to work that is anything but fragmentary. The poetry of Chaucer and Shakespeare, two writers who, when we as teachers try to enact their liveliness in schools, bear the burden of being known as great. They labour under the disadvantage of already being, unarguably, in the canon, or the Canon; of being like Grecian urns, free of our questions. In our teaching we have the duty of bringing them (happy phrase) down to earth, to where the miller lives, that fine Englishman, 'short-sholdred, brood and thikke knarree', to where Falstaff lives, to where Touchstone lives, when he tells us that 'The truest poetry is the most feigning'. Maybe there is the healing.

6

Two big guns:
Chaucer and Shakespeare

Others abide our question. Thou art free. (Matthew Arnold)

INTRODUCTION

I wanted to provide examples of work of what most people would consider to be the highest stature for children to respond to. The two big guns I chose were 'The worshipful father and first founder and embellisher of ornate eloquence in our English, I mean Master Geoffrey Chaucer' (which is what Caxton calls him), and that 'upstart crow beautified with feathers' (as Robert Greene calls Shakespeare). Here we will, I assumed, if in no other place, hear the sun singing, and help the children to hear that sun singing, too. I could have searched through Milton, but felt sure that my search would have been fruitless. Similarly, Wordsworth and Pope (who, for some, approach this kind of stature) seemed unlikely to provide much that was accessible to children. No doubt there is a reader of this book who disagrees with me, and I would be delighted to hear from anyone who can show me work by children written in the grip of these three writers (and any others, come to that).

GEOFFREY CHAUCER AND THE MILLER

The Chaucer passage I used, the description of the miller, is, of course, from 'The Prologue' to *The Canterbury Tales*. The first five lines of it is also to be found in Cotton's useful little anthology (2000). Geoffrey Chaucer lived from about 1343 to 1400, and is widely thought to be the greatest poet of Middle English, and also one of the greatest poets who have ever written in these islands. I quote the Caxton remark above because it gives a glimpse of the status Chaucer has always had in our literary history. I first discovered him when I was studying for 'A' levels at grammar school in the 1960s. My meeting his work coincided with the first inkling that my commitment to evangelical Christianity was an act of intellectual cowardice and dishonesty; Chaucer's evident lust for life and all its complications should have knocked me off my pious pedestal of moral certainty immediately, but it didn't. I wasn't brave enough to let myself tumble. Now, however, I can hear the author of *The Canterbury Tales* relishing Sir Toby Belch's hit at Malvolio in *Twelfth Night*, 2.3: 'Dost thou think because thou art virtuous there shall be no more cakes and ale?' Then, I tried, cravenly, to marry the world as it was to my pious vision of how it ought to be, and became uncomfortable for most of a lifetime as a result.

Forbidding as the scale and language of Chaucer's poetry was, parts of the work imprinted itself on my mind for ever, or at least until I forget everything. The opening can still captivate children:

Whan that Aprill with his shoures soote
The droghte of March hath perced to the roote,
And bathed every veyne in swich licour
Of which vertu engendred in the flour

(Chaucer, 'The Prologue', lines 544ff.)

Although no expert on the pronunciation of the Anglo-Norman in which these words are written, I am sure that there are two rules about reading them aloud that seem worth following. The first is, always pronounce the 'e' at the end of words, unless it is followed by another vowel. The second is, give every consonant and pair – and triplet – of consonants its full value. Try 'droghte' again, with these two rules in mind. I simply read these lines to children with confidence, and I find that convinces sufficiently. I recall Oscar Wilde's comment on quoting: anyone can quote accurately, but he said he quoted with great feeling. I apply this to my reading of Chaucer to children, and hope that there isn't an expert among the staff at the back of the room. I haven't knowingly fallen foul of one so far.

As for meaning, much can be inferred from the context and from the resemblance of Chaucer's words to modern words. It isn't difficult here to find 'sweet showers' and 'drought'; 'pierced' and 'root'; 'vein', 'such' and 'liquor' (meaning 'moisture'); 'virtue' and 'flower'. Indeed, the talking about these words with children is a painless lesson in etymology. In the following passage, 'carl' (the origin of 'Charles') means 'countryman'; Coghill renders it as 'chap', and 'bloke' might do. 'Nones' (pronounce that 'e') is 'occasion'; 'ram' is 'prize', and 'brood and thikke knarre' conveys sufficient of its meaning through its sound:

> The Miller was a stout carl for the nones;
> Full byg he was of brawn, and eek of bones;
> That proved wel, for over-al ther he cam,
> At wrastling he would have alwey the ram.
> He was short-sholdred, brood and thikke knarree

Here is a rough prose translation of the whole of this passage and several of the verses following:

> The Miller was a big bloke, brawny and bony. Good job, too: he always won the prize at wrestling. Short-shouldered, broad, a thick fellow, he could heave off a door, or break it, running at it head first. His beard was as red as a sow or a fox, and broad, like a spade. On the end of his nose he had a wart, and on the wart there was a tuft of hair, red as the bristles in a sow's ear. His nostrils were black and wide. He had a sword and shield by his side. His mouth was as great as a huge furnace. He was a brawler and a buffoon, and his jokes were mostly about sin and wickedness. He could steal corn, and treble his profit. He had a golden thumb! He wore a white coat and a blue hood. He was good on the bagpipes, and he led us out of town playing them.

I have written my own pastiches of Chaucer. Like most imitations of Chaucer, they are thin: they scrape the skin off the surface of Chaucer's intent, but nothing more. I hope, though, that they get some of the points across:

> The Postman was a nimble-footed man
> That nipped so neatly round the garden gnomes . . .

> The Teacher was a lady so precise,
> Her ticks ticked tidily, all neat and nice.
> Her flowered frock, lace collar at her throat
> And gentle eyes . . . but when you got her goat
> She'd flash lightning, and sound such awful thunder
> The classroom felt it might give up, go under . . .

The Gardener was a man who smelled of earth
And branch and bark. His hands were cut and gnarled.
He knew the name of every tree, and how
To make it thrive. He'd stand under our trees
And name their illnesses, the kinds of food
To make them better . . .

I taught this lesson first at a boys' prep school. I did not teach it well. It was the last part of a longer lesson, and therefore a kind of postscript. I read Coghill's translation, but not the first four lines of the original. The boys wrote quite well:

The postman is such a puny little fellow
He pulls his little postman's bag around as if it were 400 pounds.
He's small and thin, with a small stride with lots of footsteps . . .

                                                                        (Kieran, 11)

I was quite happy with this, but I spent much of the following evening thinking about how I might have taught the Miller passage better. A day later, I had learned my lesson. In a primary school, I approached my task with more preparation and application. I realized that I needed to make an interest in what the children would write a priority, rather than getting more examples of children's writing for this book. My lesson in the boys' school was a classic example of how tunnel-vision concentration on the product cripples the process, the teaching, which is the point. Also (and this should have been obvious) I realized that the Chaucer has to be the main core of a lesson.

I made the miller the main focus of the session, which lasted over an hour. I read the first five lines in the original, and then read Neville Coghill's translation (available in Harrison and Stuart-Clark, 1977). We discussed the way the words not only *meant* strength, vigour and coarseness, but enacted them, too, sounded like them: 'stout carl', 'big he was of braun . . . bones', 'brood and thikke knarre'. Obviously, the alliteration was important here. I asked the children if they could make some of their words *sound* like their meanings. I suggested that little delicate people required little delicate words, for example. I also asked them if they could use alliteration to help to convey their meanings. Other suggestions I made were: think about the senses. What does your subject sound like? Smell like? And so on.

The Flower Seller

The flower seller was a very pretty lady,
Her hair that was golden like the sun
Curled around her radiant face.
She was a small skinny woman
Aged about twenty three
Her face was like an angel's
But without a halo
A holy friend down from heaven
Her body was like a butterfly's
But without wings
A pretty bug floating around.
Her nose was small,
But her eyes were big
Bright blue and beautiful
Her lips were red as the roses she sold
And her voice was as clear as a bell
She wore a pretty sky blue dress
And her shoes were always clean.
As she sold her flowers she used to hum a little tune
And she liked to tell me wonderful
Stories about Mermaids in the sea
And princesses in castles.
I loved that flower seller
She impressed me with her singing voice
And the poems that she told.
I loved that flower seller.

(Gemma, 10)

Gemma took a brave decision to write about someone completely
different from the miller, and drew a word-picture of great deli-
cacy. Her grasp of subordinate clauses is beyond her years (see
especially the first three lines) and her similes ('her body was like
a butterfly's / but without wings) are surprising and right. She also
uses alliteration to some purpose: 'a holy friend down from Heaven
/ Her body . . .', for example. She uses a telling oxymoron well
('pretty bug'). In contrast, a boy composed the following:

The man's a wall of stone
His clothes were blue and green
As large as a house

The flower seller

The flower seller was a very pretty lady,
Her hair that was golden like the sun
curled around her ~~face~~ raidiant face.
She was a small skinny woman
Aged about twenty three
Her face was like an angel's
But without a halo
A holy friend down from heaven
Her Body was like a butterfly's
But without wings
A pretty bug floating around.
Her nose was small,
But her eyes were big
Bright blue and beautiful
Her lips were red as the roses she sold
And her voice was as clear as a bell
She wore a pretty sky blue dress
and her shoes were allways clean.
As she sold her flowers she used to hum a little tune
And she liked to tell me wonderful
Stories about Mermaids in the sea
And princesses in castles.
I loved that flower seller
She impressed me withe her singing voice
And the poems that she told.
I loved that flower seller

By Gemma

He could lift the heaviest weights.
His face was like an ugly sister
He had a little trick:
He would back into a wall
And you would have a print of him on the wall.

(Daniel, 10)

This piece was scribed for Daniel by his headteacher, who shows more commitment than many seem to do to the children and their learning. The writer, who had problems too many and personal to go into here, was visibly encouraged by his headteacher's help, and by the praise he got from the staff and myself for his vivid piece. He had taken a hint from me: the miller's ability to run at a door and break it with his head had led to his lines about the wall.

Here are some of the other pieces written on this afternoon, when Chaucer was in the school with me, the children and the staff, and when something creative was in the air; it was an afternoon when we behaved confidently, and believed in ourselves, and discarded for a couple of hours the guinea of league tables, and went joyously for the heavenly host:

The smelly baby
with rosy red cheeks
and grey-green eyes
a smelly 6 week old nappy
and a splodged stained bib
a screaming voice
and a weight of 23 packets of jelly babies.
His favourite trick is
to burp the alphabet.
Like a rat in baby's clothing
he squeals and squeals for the last bit of apple sauce.
A broken radio on legs
he screeches for a cuddle.
At five in the morning
THE LITTLE MONSTER'S ASLEEP!

(Lucy, 10)

Don't underestimate my little sis.
She's like a bear, cute but tough.
Her oval glasses make her look sweet and innocent

But behind closed doors beware
Don't underestimate my little sis.

Her blonde hair and medium size nose,
Her clothes are hip hop and cool.
She likes her stories with added blood and gore.
Behind closed doors beware
Don't underestimate my little sis.

Her school reports are always good
So are mine, I might add
My mum at home and dad are always proud
Behind closed doors beware
Don't underestimate my little sis.

She loves to sing All Saints songs
But a saint
She aint!
Behind closed doors beware
Don't underestimate my little sis.

(Lauren, 10)

I watched one girl write most of her piece, as she was lying belly-down on the floor next to where I was based much of the time. Her pen hardly left the paper as she worked:

The woman, tall as the Eiffel Tower, had a gaunt face as white as snow. Her lips were outlined with red lipstick.

Millicent's hair was black as ebony and her nose made her appear bird-like.

A fur hat was perched on her head which made her look even taller. A long draping coat of fresh fur hung on her shoulders. She walked like a robin.

Her main talent was telling people off, shouting at them in disgust. She looked as if anyone hit her she would snap, she looked so fragile, but behind her skinny arms were muscles as hard as steel. She enjoyed eating mints and once she got down to the last bit she'd spit it out at people. She wasn't that popular because of her behaviour and often got drunk in the pub. Her voice was like a raspy wind escaping her mouth. She'd screech at anyone who was doing anything wrong like dropping litter, even though she did it herself.

(Katy, 11)

As Cotton (2000) suggests in his book, two other passages would lend themselves being read to children, about a knight and a prioress:

> A Knight ther was, and that a worthy man,
> That fro the tyme that he first bigan
> To ryden out, he loved chivalrye,
> Trouthe and honour, freedom and courteiyse

> She was so charitable and so pitous
> She wold wepe, if that she sawe a mous
> Caught in a trappe, if it were dede or bledde.
> Of smale houndes had she, that she fedde
> With rosted flesh, or milk and wastel bred.
> [pitous = compassionate; wastel = finest]

SHAKESPEARE

Introduction

I have written before about teaching Shakespeare to young children. I still find that teachers and others say: 'You can't teach Shakespeare without teaching his historical context'; 'Surely you must use simplified language'; 'I have written my own version of *A Midsummer Night's Dream* for my class to act'. For an attempted refutation of all the notions that hover behind remarks like these, see my book (1999b). I will say here that I am sure that the historical context needs to be taught after, and as a poor second to, the language. It is, after all, the language that has caused Shakespeare's name to survive, like Jonson's 'bright star', illuminating infinite numbers of nights, in theatres and studies, down the centuries. The historical context will sometimes shed a little extra glimmer on that language, but when it becomes more important in classrooms than the language, damage is done to Shakespeare's work and to the children's education.

As far as the difficulty argument is concerned, there are many passages of Shakespeare that do not present intractable linguistic problems to children. For a list to start with, see Sedgwick, 1999, pp. 149–50. Further, to teach a version of Shakespeare that we have written, concentrating on the plot, is not to teach Shakespeare at all. He is not there in his plots, most of which he lifted from various sources. He is only there in the language. I will merely add here a quotation from W. H. Auden (1977), who attacked in a 1933 review what he called 'the bunk in most teaching of Shakespeare, with its concentration on characters and plot, and its omission of the poetry'.

I have included some autobiographical accounts in each chapter in this book. For my Shakespeare chapter, I need some words I have already published (1999b) which I revise here. I met Sir John Falstaff some time in 1960 in a chalky, dusty classroom in a South London grammar school:

> FALSTAFF: Now Hal, what time of day is it, lad?
> PRINCE: Thou art so fat-witted, with drinking of old sack, and unbuttoning thee after supper, and sleeping upon benches after noon, that thou hast forgotten to demand what truly thou would'st truly know . . .
>
> (*Henry IV*, Part 1:I:2)

and I immediately liked him. Later, his prose hatchet job on the concept of honour, in the same play, made me laugh out loud – as it still does. ('Honour hath no skill in surgery then? No. What is honour? A word . . . Who hath it? He that died 'a Wednesday'.) Many years later I was to read Robert Nye's extraordinary novel *Falstaff* (1977) which, along with Anthony Burgess's *Nothing Like the Sun* (1964), presents a vivid and alarming twentieth-century fictional commentary on Shakespeare's sheer fecundity. While studying *Henry IV*, I saw John Stride as Prince Hal at the Old Vic (Tony Britton should have been Hotspur, but he had been injured the night before in a sword fight with Hal, and that heightened my new passion: they actually fought, and got hurt!). I don't remember who was Falstaff. I watched my little brother, then 14 years old, play Gertrude at school to Hywel Bennett's Hamlet, potentially, I now reflect, a Freudian nightmare. Then, through my experiences as an enjoyer of Shakespeare, as an amateur actor, as a play-goer and occasional local radio critic, as a radio-listener, occasionally as a television-watcher, and as a reader, I have developed an enthusiasm that is really a passion.

I acted Second Servant at college in *King Lear*, watching Cornwall gouge out Gloucester's eyes. I had to pop little round capsules of red stuff against Gloucester's cheeks. Unreliable memory tells me now that this was Gordon Moore's cosmetic toothpaste, which was advertised regularly on Radio Luxembourg. I wrote a poem about this experience:

Student Actors, 1966
(for John Cotton)

He tucks twenty Players
    in his robes.
His eyelids flicker,
    tenser than shells
as Make-up dabs swan's-
    egg green on them.

On stage First Servant
    pops and plasters
blood in the grizzled beard.
    Cornwall puts
his foot down. Gloucester's
    thrust out to 'smell
His way to Dover'.
    They end each scene,
like the blinded duke,
    facing 'knowledge
of themselves'; and dying
    for a smoke.

(Based on *King Lear* III:7:55–97; IV:5:272)

My friend Richard (First Servant) had, in rehearsal, died like a
starfish, flat on his back, horribly comic, until the director, the head
of the English Department, showed him how stabbed people die
('Like this! They crumple!'). He gripped his belly and twisted and
squirmed to the ground. He lay there for a few seconds and looked
up: 'Like that!' I recall wondering how he knew this. I have
collected Hamlets (Olivier, of course, with his pageboy hair-do);
some bloke at OUDS seriously upstaged by Jonathan James-Moore
as a fascist Claudius; Ian McKellen, Michael Pennington, Martin
Marquez (from *The Bill*). I have regretted missing others (especially
Jonathan Pryce). I have puzzled over those love affairs in the
sonnets: that beautiful young man, that lady whose eyes 'are
nothing like the sun'. I have laughed with and at Falstaff, recogniz-
ing, sometimes, elements of myself in him: 'I would it were bedtime, Hal, and all well'; 'Come, mistress, my breakfast, come / Oh
I could wish this tavern were my drum' (*Henry IV*, Part 1).

I have found that many people's experience of Shakespeare was
less positive than mine. I am grateful for what I had.

Although the teaching of Shakespeare is semi-official in the

United Kingdom, this only goes as far as certain plays, notably, at Key Stage 2, *Romeo and Juliet*. Also, various versions of the tales of Shakespeare, by writers like Geraldine McCoughrean have become semi-official too in teachers' desperation to gain some purchase on the teaching of Shakespeare. So have countless textbooks of variable quality on Shakespeare's life, the Globe and his contemporary theatre. All this work merely skirts the edge of the central issue, which is Shakespeare's language and the related issue of how children learn from it.

The Tempest

Here is an example of that language and that learning. 'Full Fathom Five' is a song sung by Ariel in *The Tempest*, 1,2:

> Full Fathom Five thy father lies,
> Of his bones are coral made;
> Those are pearls that were his eyes;
> Nothing of him that doth fade,
> But doth suffer a sea-change
> Into something rich and strange.
> Sea-nymphs hourly ring his knell.
> Hark, now I hear them, 'ding-dong bell'.

I played a record of this song as performed on 'Songs and Dances from Shakespeare' by the Broadside Band directed by Jeremy Barlow. The poem may have troubled the children. After all, it is about the death of a father, one of the most important rites of passage that human beings experience. 'I became mortal the night my father died' Dannie Abse tells us (Abse, 1970, p. 83). The risk of troubling children should never discourage us from talking about the big guns of human experience, as long as we talk with honesty and integrity. When I asked the children to write, however, I took the heat out of the setting by suggesting that children wrote about toys and other precious possessions that they had lost. I pointed out the alliteration in the Shakespeare:

> Caring cuddly Cuddles
> plunges into the
> deep water losing
> his softness. All
> because of the

swirling dark water.
Lobsters snip the
stitches. Each half
says goodbye.
Old wide eyes
have now become
dull small pebbles.
The fish's tail
swishes it to
another dark place
where an octopus
bites his ears
and eats them.
All of a
sudden a shark
eats my teddy
and I cry
and I cry
and I cry.

(Rachel, 11)

My magical marvellous box moves marvellously,
endlessly to the coral sea bed.
The hinges turn to anemones,
stuck onto ruby red rocks.
Magic paper slides away from magic words.
They become shrimps and fishes
ploughing through the water.
Its open top transforms
to an open-mouthed shark,
hiding under the stand.
The leather changes to dead coral
floating like debris
from rippling rubbish
from wrecked riots of ships.
The now brown bronze
wanders into caves
and turns into fish
too hard to see.
My precious, priceless possessions
run away in gusts of foam.

(Helen, 9)

Ring

My ring, ring, beautiful ring sinks to the seabed,
the sea knocking out the glittering stones.
The sea snaps the stones to glittering blue sands.
The silver circle that holds it is now rust.
Tiny, tiny little fish dart in and out as if it were an adventure
    playground for fish,
Lost, never seen again for eternity.

(Louise, 9)

My Rosy Rosary

My rosy rosary takes a rough ride
down to the ocean deep.

It plunges to a ship, wrecked on a rock,
so humbly cracked.

Fish swipe and quarrel over the onyx stone
that once linked a holy object.

The bronze figure of a man that was once Jesus
will rust like an old copper pipe

and the cross that held him will mould and rot away.

My rosy rosary takes a rough ride
down to the ocean deep.

(Giuliano, 10)

In *The Tempest*, the savage Caliban has many of the most beautiful
lines, such as these:

Be not afear'd, the isle is full of noises,
Sounds and sweet airs, that give delight and hurt not.
Sometimes a thousand twangling instruments
Will hum about mine ears; and sometimes voices,
That if I then had waked after long sleep,
Will make me sleep again; and then in dreaming,
The clouds methought would open, and show riches
Ready to drop upon me, that when I waked
I cried to dream again.

The Tempest (3:2:130ff)

When I teach this passage, I suggest that the children concentrate on the five senses, including taste and smell, which are usually neglected, and which, as in this next piece, can add so much to writing:

> Be not afeared, the isle is full of sparkles
> from sky, land and sea.
> Waterfalls splash into crystal rivers
> and turn into the ocean.
> Smells of spices, sweet flowers, salty waters
> work their way through white deserted beaches.
> Tongue-piercing fruits
> fall through rough-jawed creatures.
> Unusual shapes hide their bodies,
> silently growing, watching the world change.
> Amethysts drop into little nooks and plop
> quietly on to the ground.
>
> (Helen, 11)

Other writers in the same school wrote about 'the rich salt sea, wild and refreshing' and 'waterfalls splashing as they hit the shimmering water'. I made a resolution that, on the next occasion that I met them, I would remind them of Caliban's speech and their writing, and introduce them to the old American folk song 'The Big Rock Candy Mountain', which is about a world similar to the island Caliban inherits, and which the children themselves have described:

> In the Big Rock Candy Mountain
> You never change your socks,
> And little streams of alcohol
> Come trickling down the rocks.
>
> In the Big Rock Candy Mountain
> There's a land that's fair and bright,
> Where the hand-outs grow on bushes
> And you sleep out every night.
>
> In the Big Rock Candy Mountain
> The jails are made of tin
> And you can bust right out again
> As soon as they put you in.

I also intend to introduce the children to another, similar world where:

> The wolf also shall dwell with the lamb, and the leopard shall lie down with the kid; and the calf and the young lion and the fatling together; and a little child shall lead them. And the lion shall eat straw like the ox. And the sucking child shall play on the hole of the asp, and the weaned child shall put his hand on the cockatrice's den. They shall not hurt or destroy in all my holy mountain.

(Isaiah 11:9)

King Lear

It is relatively easy to introduce children to plays like *Romeo and Juliet*, *A Midsummer Night's Dream* and, as above, *The Tempest*. However, I wanted to help children to write by using a play that is not usually considered suitable for young children. *King Lear* is way beyond most children's ken. Its central themes of filial ingratitude and of knowledge coming only with old age and suffering (and even blindness and madness) mean that it is rarely taught to young children. Its discussion of nihilism – the words 'never' and 'nothing' chime forlornly throughout the play – make it forbidding for many adults. But here is an entry point for children in primary schools. As Lear descends into madness, while simultaneously rising into self-knowledge, he meets Edgar, son of the Duke of Gloucester, who is pretending to be mad. Edgar says that he is:

> Poor Tom, that eats the swimming frog; the toad, the tadpole, the wall-newt, and the water; that in the fury of his heart, when the foul fiend rages, eats cow-dung for salads, swallows the old rat and the ditch-dog; drinks the green mantle of the standing pool; who is whipped from tithing to tithing, and stock-punished, and imprisoned; who hath three suits to his back, six shirts to his body,
>
> > Horse to ride, and weapon to wear;
> > But mice and rats and such small deer
> > Have been Tom's food for seven long year.
>
> Beware my follower. Peace, Smulkin! peace, thou fiend.

(King Lear 3:4:115ff)

I wrote a version of this, quickly, in a notebook that I carry everywhere, while the children were finishing another task. This was partly to demonstrate that you don't have to be Shakespeare or a child in school to write, or *have* to write. This is a useful lesson to teach as often as possible in this practical way because, by our normal practice, students learn implicitly that only great artists and prisoners in schools write, or *have* to write. Also, my writing (thin and extremely derivative as it is) provided a useful de-Bardifying, un-Swanning bridge between the Shakespeare passage and the children's work:

> Poor man, that drinks discarded ale from tankards in pub gardens; that greets girls with blown kisses, boys with wavings of his wet fists; who burrows like a rat in waste bins, searching for butts of cigarettes; who is chased from the gardens with the curses and cries of the privileged sane sailing behind him; who, in his innocent lunacy, splashes, smacking the water of the village duckpond, raucously and rancorously denouncing the rancid deacons of the local church . . . Poor man, that once sat in pews, in a jury box, on a hill gazing down at the Gloucestershire hills . . .
>
> Have a kind of peace, thinks this passer-by, dropping palm-warm pence into your hat. Have a kind of peace, and a fresh cigarette, and a half of some golden ale.

The children wrote:

> Poor old Bertie Saggot, eating the odd half-eaten apple or the occasionally chewed sandwich, the few pence in his moth-eaten pocket don't come to much. His beard's grown longer and longer and has got grubbier and grubbier as the days have gone on, his dark eyes bloodshot by the car fumes. His broken leg curled under the ragged cloth covering his limp body. His long mousy hair tickled his big blunt nose that hung over his mouth, filled with yellow and black teeth like gravestones. He sleeps most of the long day and prowls the street at night for maybe a half drink of beer in the dustbin behind the restaurants.
>
> (Emily, 10)

> Poor Bob.
> who sits on the sea wall,
> sleeps under the dinghies

and wraps himself in sails.
Sometimes a mob hit him with oars.
he chews on odd bits of rope
and gnaws on sponges.

(Tom, 10)

Poor old Betty who eats mouldy bread and rotten cabbages, wears old ragged clothes full of holes, a red shawl round her bare shoulders. She holds out a cup and begs. She drinks rain water from the puddles. She sleeps in doorways. At night she limps through the dirty streets trying to find shelter. Her brown face is covered in scabs and wrinkles. Her straggly brown hair falls around her. Her long skinny legs have mud spattered up them.

(Marion, 10)

How much this 'innocent' writer (Emily) already knows! These children go to a middle-class village school, and the casual observer might presume they would have a kind of innocence of the darker side of the world, but that observer would be wrong, as we can see. Tom is not a fluent writer, but look at his alliteration and assonance, and his appropriately blunt depiction of his character. Very often, I find that children who are labelled as 'less able', or (these days) 'in need of learning support', respond to Shakespeare with a less wordy bluntness than their A-stream friends manage, and that their style feels right in the context.

Finally, I was asked to help some children write about Christmas. I read the children this passage from *King Lear* again, playing with it as usual, so that the children got the feel, the taste of the words, so that they began their jobs as Shakespearean critics (in Steiner's terms: performance is primary criticism). It was suitable for Christmas because it worked so hard against the rest of the preparations in the school: the tree, the mock presents under it, the tinsel, the sentimental travesty of the gospel story, the sugary songs about little donkeys and little drummer boys, the ghastly displays of the Holy Family in the assembly hall. When I read the children's pieces afterwards, I felt that Jack and Charlie, like Poor Tom in *King Lear*, had a more rightful place in the gospel story than many of the accretions that have stuck on to it over the past two centuries, especially that damn' donkey and that damn' drummer boy:

Poor Jack
all alone at night
that drinks the rain
that waits outside the shops for someone to come by
that wakes in the middle of the night
hearing voices of foxes and owls
that looks through the bins for food.
He has nearly no clothes
that begs and begs for peoples money
that has no-one to talk to
that talks to himself when he is lonely
that cries at night for food
no-one to say goodnight
or to stop and say hello
no-one to look after him when he's ill.
No-one cares about poor Jack
that writes letters to himself for company
that has no family and no friends
that wanders around the streets at night
that tries to do his best to make friends

(Gemma, 10)

Poor Charlie drinks out of puddles. He raids the bin and eats the scraps. He sleeps in a cardboard box in an alleyway. He gets bitten by stray dogs. He gets clawed by stray cats. Poor Charlie gets rejected. He has no friends because he is different. He wears an old grey coat he found in a dump, a shirt with a dozen holes. Poor old Charlie.

(Rebekah, 10)

As You Like It

One of the easiest entry points comes in Act 2, Scene 7 of *As You Like It*. I have written about teaching this speech before (Sedgwick, 1999b, pp. 73ff) but in this current chapter I take the work a little further. I have just heard a fine production of this play on the radio, but was struck as usual how the actor playing Jaques (in this case the excellent Nicholas le Prevost) always finds it impossible to come into the conversation with the famous lines beginning 'All's the world's a stage' with anything like a natural approach. I performed these lines – hammed them up, I suppose – to a group of middle school children who were on a course for young writers:

All the world's a stage,
And all the men and women merely players.
They have their exits and their entrances;
And one man in his time plays many parts,
His acts being ages seven. At first the infant,
Mewling and puking in the nurse's arms;
Then the whining schoolboy, with his satchel
And shining morning face, creeping like snail
Unwillingly to school. And then the lover,
Sighing like furnace, with a woeful ballad
Made to his mistress' eyebrow. Then a soldier,
Full of strange oaths, and bearded like the pard,
Jealous in honour, sudden and quick in quarrel,
Seeking the bubble reputation
Even in the cannon's mouth. And then the justice,
In fair round belly with good capon lin'd,
With eyes severe and beard of formal cut,
Full of wise saws and modern instances;
And so he plays his part. The sixth age shifts
Into the lean and slippered pantaloon,
With spectacles on nose and pouch on side,
His youthful hose, well sav'd, a world too wide
For his shrunk shank; and his big manly voice,
Turning again towards childish treble, pipes
And whistles in his sound. Last scene of all,
That ends this strange eventful history,
Is second childishness and mere oblivion;
Sans teeth, sans eyes, sans taste, sans everything.

(*As You Like It*, 2:7:139ff)

I explained some difficult terms, such as 'pard' (leopard), 'woeful ballad / Made to his mistress' eyebrow', and 'sans', and then we performed the speech together, muling and puking early on, whining with an aged treble at the end, and with a full gamut of vocal sounds in between: sentimental lover, marching soldier (note how his lines, from 'Full of strange oaths, and bearded like the pard' march across the lines) and pompous justice, whose belly has been lined with castrated cockerels, traditionally bribes.

I asked the children to work in groups and write their own version: not of the whole speech, but of a chosen section. Certain parts of the speech – the schoolchild and the old man – appealed to the writers more than the others:

The baby crying, weeping for its rattle, pink and blue,
whinging for a drop of warm milk ready from the microwave,
but then, when night falls, peace, quiet, until . . .

The schoolchild mopes mournfully to school
scuffing hated school shoes in despair
turning up the road to imprisonment.

The schoolchild, quiet when he wants to be
and loud and noisy when he doesn't
dawdling to school as though he has all the time in the world
and making silly excuses when confronted . . .
being forced to enter lessons
answering reluctantly the register,
secretly rolling up her skirt
being shouted out: 'Skirt on the knee!'

The lovers, committed, connected on their wedding day
flirting along all night, all day,
growing too old, but will they stay
forever, forever, till death do us part?

The businessman, smartly dressed and ready for a day's work,
His schedule neatly typed, his meetings listed,
His desk neat, all his equipment organised.

The door to door salesman dragging his display case,
his crafty smile and pleasant convincing tone
as he flogs off his goods to his unsuspecting victims.

The landlord of a pub calling for last orders again,
yelling, GO AWAY, IT'S CLOSING TIME AT LAST!,
pushing the grumbling drunks out of the door.

The old wrinkled man with low voice breaks back to infant's voice.

The old man, bedridden and dreaming
about his younger days sighs his last breath

The old man sits in his dressing gown
watching UK Gold replays.

The use of modern diction in response to Shakespeare's diction –
'microwave', 'UK Gold replays', 'Skirt on the knee!', 'schedule
neatly typed, his meetings listed' – helps children to demystify
Shakespeare's words. It helps them to 'de-Bardify', to 'un-Swan'
Shakespeare's words, to relate his unfamiliar words to their familiar
words. This in turn is likely to help them to make Shakespeare
theirs, rather than the possession of some powerful hegemony
presided over by, say, Prince Charles and the chairmen and chair-
women of the examining boards. It enables them, for example, to
link Jaques' words with their own words; to build a bridge between
Shakespeare's language and their own language. Bardolatry and
Swanning will never build that bridge.

This is not to devalue Shakespeare's words. Activities like this
do not take Shakespeare's words away from children. Those words
are there to be returned to when the children have interpreted
them in terms of their words, and in terms of their own worlds.
And the children are more likely to return to Shakespeare's words
when they have had the opportunity to play with them in their
own active way.

This exercise has also enabled children to refer to their own lives
and tribulations: discipline in school, for example. They also reflect
on their futures: 'but will they stay forever, forever, till death do us
part?'. Much good creative writing is a kind of rehearsal for life,
and here the lines about the young lovers seem especially poignant.
I have written before (Sedgwick, 1999b, p. 75) how writers using
this passage 'seem to be reflecting wryly on their own memories
and current lives'.

The Rose of Youth

One single line from Shakespeare often sets children off on unpre-
dictable writing adventures. During these adventures, they work
with both their own obsessions and with Shakespeare's lines. I
have written about this extensively in my 1999 book on Shakespeare. Here I will merely quote one line, chosen because it comes
from another play that no one would normally think of sharing
with young children (or older ones, too, come to that). I hope that I
have shown throughout this book that we need not restrict our
teaching to passages of English literature that were expressly
written for children. The line is 'He wears the rose of youth upon
him' from *Antony and Cleopatra*. These children have simply used
the structure of that line to write their lines:

She waves the flag of innocence above her.

He carries the heavy ball of death behind him.

She drips the tears of agony down her face.

She wraps the robe of wisdom about her.

He carries the daisy of age in his hand.

She carries the clover of life in her head.

She pulls the boulder of fear behind her.

He holds the flower of love close to him.

She clutches the violet of love close to her chest.

She holds the yolk of hate to her heart.

Spells

When my friend John Cotton had read my earlier book on Shakespeare (Sedgwick, 1999b), he pointed out to me that the witches in *Macbeth* had set a bad example for spells. Ever since he said this, I have asked children to study 'Double double, toil and trouble', and then to write a spell to make beautiful things happen. (I will not reprint the Shakespeare here because it is readily available.) But the children wrote poems in the grip of that speech, that turned the witches' message beautifully on its head:

Blue from the rainbow gently falling
Come to my cauldron lovely dreams
Sun from the sky happily dreaming
Come to my pot where you can awake
Bubble bubble no more trouble
Come to my cauldron where you will stay
Deep red ruby come from your cave
And join me in my bubbling bath
Bright rainbow from the darkness
Come and dance along with me
Bubble bubble no more trouble

Young rainbow look for Mummy
Yummy lovely you'll find her in here
Strand of baby's soft silk hair
Come and burn and turn to ashes
Bubble bubble no more trouble
Come to my cauldron where you will stay
Stir it up until it boils
No more moans and no more complaints

(Jasmine, 10)

Bright Inspector

I finish with oxymorons. They are essential to Shakespeare but not essential, it would seem, to modern speech. The bridge is built here from Shakespeare' side. An oxymoron is:

a figure of speech in which contradictory terms are brought together in what is at first sight an impossible combination ... [examples are] 'I burn and freeze like ice' [and] the 'darkness visible' of Hell in Milton's *Paradise Lost*. (Gray, 1984)

The word comes from the Greek words for sharp and dull. There are oxymorons of a kind in *Timon of Athens*, 4:3:

Thus much of this will make black white, foul fair,
Wrong right, base noble, old young, coward valiant.

Gibson (1992), in his edition of *Romeo and Juliet* for schools, points out that 'much of [that] play is about the clash of opposites' and that therefore 'oxymorons are particularly appropriate'. I have listed a group of Romeo's and Juliet's oxymorons in Sedgwick (1999b). It is probably enough to give eleven examples here:

brawling love, loving hate, heavy lightness, feather of lead, bright smoke, cold fire, sick health, beautiful tyrant, fiend angelical, damned saint, honourable villain

I wrote down some oxymorons of my own:

soft nail, deep lawn, weighty cloud, feline reindeer, hot moon, sweet pain, gentle glare, heated glacier, doubtful faith, miser-

able optimist, tedious excitement, dull radiance, immaculately
derelict

Some oxymorons seem to have entered the language, like 'glad
rags'. Oxymorons are useful for young writers because, by their
nature, they prevent cliché. Although, as Fowler (1965) says, they
can become absurd ('that's terribly sweet of you') they train children in looking for the unconventional, the surprising, the paradox-
ical. Also study of the oxymorons that they produce throws up
interesting issues, such as why some oxymorons don't seem as
contradictory as we thought at first.

I asked young writers to identify what is going on in those
oxymorons from Shakespeare and then in my own examples.
Somebody noticed that each line was made up of 'opposites'. I took
this further and introduced the technical word 'oxymoron'. The
children then simply listed all the oxymorons that they could think
of, chose their favourites and made them into little 'oxymoronic
poems'. In doing this, they were, as Initial Teacher Training
National Curriculum Secondary English puts it 'gain[ing] an
appreciation of Shakespeare's language, including its poetic
qualities':

Black light
that
brightly fades
with creative destruction
and destructive peace.
Silent thunder
that
strikes quietly.

(Anon., 11)

Flying submarine
that
slowly speeds
over
black snow
in the white night.

(Anon., 11)

Oxymorons are surprising. They can trip the writer into truth, into a sense of the heavenly host, which (unlike a guinea) is not necessarily a rational, composed, unfragmented thing.

Finally, a poem written after this boy had studied Demetrius' lines: 'O Helen, goddess, nymph . . .' (*A Midsummer Night's Dream*, 3:2:137–44):

An Over-the-top Love Poem

Oh my dear lovely lady
how come someone as beautiful as you
has no wedded husband?

Your eyes are so dark,
the summer night looks as light as the clouds.
Your skin is as light
as the lightest sun.
The other ladies around here
look like the colour of swamps
compared to you.
You must be
the most greatest lady lover
in the world.
Surely there can't be better.

(Anon, 9)

Among other passages that I have used in primary schools, the following are the most successful:

Cymbeline 4:2:268–75, 'Fear no more the heat o' the sun'.
Henry IV Part 1 1:2:1–9, 'Thou art so fat-witted' (and all other insults: see Hill and Ottchen, 1994).
King Lear 3:2:1–7, 'Blow, winds, and crack your cheeks!'.
A Midsummer Night's Dream 3:1: 87–94, 'I'll follow you'; 5:1:349–68 'Now the hungry lion roars'.
Richard II 3:3:147–55, 'I'll give my jewels for a set of beads'; 1:4:53–93, 'O then I see Queen Mab hath been with you'; 3:2:75, 'O serpent heart'.

See my book (Sedgwick, 1999b) for details of all these lessons.

I hope and believe that, through the work described in this chapter, both 'the worshipful father and first founder and embellisher of our English' and the 'upstart crow beautified with feathers' have begun to live in the experience of young children; that, in living there, they have helped the children to grow as true writers and true critics: people alert to parts of their tradition, without which they would be lesser human beings.

In similar ways, children will be lesser human beings if they don't have the opportunity to face up to religious writing.

Creativity and the Creation

A Poet's affair is with God, to whom he is accountable, and of whom is his reward. (Robert Browning, letter to John Ruskin, quoted in Jacobs, 1997)

And God saw that it was good. (Genesis 1)

INTRODUCTION

Dylan Thomas (whose Saviour was 'Rarer than radium') replied (or so it is said) to an American journalist who had asked the obvious question: 'These poems are written for the love of man and in praise of God, and I'd be a damn' fool if they weren't.' He later placed these words, with their potent mixture of the numinous and the profane, in a note at the beginning of his *Collected Poems* (1952). God shines in Thomas' poems. The Argentinean poet and short-story writer, Jorge Luis Borges (in Robson, 1973), also yoked his work to God or, more accurately, he found it was yoked there: 'We must . . . let the Holy Ghost, or the Muse, or the subconscious . . . have its way with us.' The Australian poet, Les Murray, adds another dimension to this connection between 'love of man' and 'praise of God' by dedicating most of his collections of poetry 'To the glory of God' (for example, *Dog Fox Field* (1991b).

Prayers and poetry have much in common, because both are searches for the truth, sometimes ardent, unremitting and determined, and sometimes cool and almost lifeless. Murray quotes a wonderful remark of Huckleberry Finn: 'You can't pray a lie' and comments that 'you can't poe one either' ('Poetry and Religion' in *Collected Poems*, 1991a). Simone Weil writes somewhere that, if in the search for truth you turn away from Christ, you will eventually fall into his arms 'because he is the truth'.

I have written earlier in this book that I am more interested in the process through which children go when they write than the product which they aim to make. This is especially relevant in a chapter about religion and writing, because the religious or spiritual life is essentially, conventionally but truthfully enough, a pilgrimage. In Chapter 4 on fragments, I wrote about my own pilgrimage – from a fundamentalist-influenced young man to a mature man who saw the world as a baffling collection of shifting images of which he had a duty to make, through his writing, some kind of sense. If one still held the views of a fundamentalist, one would see the religious life as entirely product-oriented: one is marching to heaven and, as Jim Reeves famously sang, 'this world is not my own, I'm just a-passing through'. Heaven, for Reeves, is the great objective, and the process of living is simply preparation for Heaven. If one accepts that truth is more complicated, however, the process becomes more interesting. It becomes, in fact the only subject.

R. S. Thomas deplored the modern obsession with technology, but even more he deplored the 'awful atheism' that seemed to him (as it does to me) to deny the possibility of a life that is not tangible, not measurable, not subject to behavioural analysis. Few poets are conventional Christians. Maybe a reason for this is suggested to us by a sad little note in Hamilton (1994) that says of the poet Rosemary Tonks, 'Since converting to evangelical Christianity in the early 1970s, she has ceased to publish.' Perhaps Tonks abandoned a search for truth, a pilgrimage, because she found it; a truth (a dubious one as far as I am concerned) that requires no more searching. Utter certainty will always be a poor position for a poet to find herself in: the greatest Christian poets (Gerard Manley Hopkins is a fine example) express sublimely the doubts that are natural: 'Mine, O thou lord of life, send my roots rain' (in Gardner, 1948).

But, on the other hand, it seems to be difficult for a poet to be an atheist,* because all poets know that the guinea matters as nothing (take no notice of the conversations you overhear when they are talking in the pub or in the restaurant about their lousy royalties) compared to the sun singing – perhaps about the Holy Ghost, perhaps about the Muse, perhaps about the subconscious.

To be explicit, what poetry (like all art) has in common with

---

* After I wrote this (December 2000) I read of the death of the poet Adrian Henri – a 'confirmed atheist' his obituarist said. His affair was not with God.

religion is a search for the centre, and an attempt to make the all too evidently ephemeral permanent. 'So long as men can breathe or eyes can see, / So long lives this, and this gives life to thee' Shakespeare famously writes, of the relationship between his poetry (and, in particular, this sonnet) and the young man whom he loves. Andrew Motion put this point and an allied one when he told Joan Bakewell of the *Independent* (24 December 2000) that:

> art – and writing in particular – can have therapeutic, salubrious and humanising values – forces even – in much the same way orthodox religion can . . . there is something to do with the idea of permanence in art which is sympathetic to the sense religious people have of wanting to find a continuing, defining shape in things.

LIVING FROM HAND TO MOUTH: THE ALTERNATIVE

Human beings have been trying, of course, to understand their nature, origins and destiny for centuries. Beyond the first known systematized attempts, there existed millions of individuals, thousands of tribes who looked at the stars and into their own natures and relationships, and reflected on them. Goethe was probably writing of Ancient Greece when he wrote that 'he who cannot draw on three thousand years is living from hand to mouth'. He might, though, have been thinking of the Arabian, Ancient Egyptian and Chinese civilizations, to name just three more. Mechanistic thinkers cannot understand this quest for understanding, because their minds are set entirely in the present, and on the observable. The past (especially) and the future are blanks to them.

The principal of one College of Further Education asked me why English and Philosophy couldn't be 'brought up to date, like psychology has been'. By psychology, he meant behaviourist psychology, a psychology that looks entirely (as far as schools are concerned) at children's behaviour in particular settings, usually little rooms a long way from their classrooms and their playgrounds, and on their answers to tests. He said, 'At least you can see what you are looking for when you test children.' I should have replied that he was like a man who had lost a pound coin under a tree in the dark. Because he couldn't see anything there, he chose to look under another tree, the grass under which was brightened by a lamp-post.

This is living from hand to mouth. It is a desperate search under a false light. To act as if there is no wisdom in Confucius, say, and Jesus, and Socrates, and Akhenaten, is to scrabble under a brightly lit tree where nothing will be found, except the debris of one century, a heap of images not worth breaking. By contrast, the religion and humanism of the last three millennia help children to see into themselves and their realities; help them to understand that, as another philosopher has written, 'the unexamined life is not worth living'. Looking at religion and humanism then helps children to examine their lives.

I have an interest in children and religion and, like everything else in this book, it has grown from my own life. Or from (they are not quite the same thing) my autobiography. I was brought up by an agnostic father, and a mother who had inherited an Irish Presbyterian background but who did not go to church. My little brother and I were sent to Sunday School when we were young, and the church chosen (for geographical reasons, presumably, though maybe my mother had done some research into the matter), happened to be an Evangelical Baptist one.

I 'went forward' at a Billy Graham meeting. This meant responding to Graham's call to those who felt that Jesus was calling them that night. They should 'come forward, come forward right now, get up out of your seats and just come forward to the front, where someone will be waiting to help you'. Actually, this event happened at a local Baptist church, not mine, where the Billy Graham Wembley Crusade meeting was being relayed. I remember the Scottish minister, Revd Angus ——, fading out the big emotional hymn – 'Just as I am', or 'Softly and tenderly Jesus is calling' or whatever – to tell us that 'This relay had cost a lost of money, and there would be buckets at the back of the church if we felt able, etc etc . . .'.

That going forward meant that I was confessing to all around me that I was a sinner ('all have sinned and come short of the glory of God'), who trusted in the saving power of Christ now that I had taken him into my heart as my Personal Saviour. I gave my testimony to the local youth group – called Christian Endeavour – as I am giving my testimony now. I was later baptized, fully immersed, when I was 16 on my profession of faith. I have been searching ever since – while, at that strange time, I thought I had found the truth.

Now I am an Anglo-Catholic with frightening agnostic tendencies. I distrust the events recounted above as much as my most sceptical reader, but I know that there is something more important than the cash nexus, than the profit motive, than the love of money. It was the Thatcher years that taught me this. W. C. Fields famously said that a woman had driven him to drink, and he forgot to say thank you. Thatcher drove me back to God. The Blair years (Thatcher years, of course, by a different name) go on teaching it to me. And my way of understanding this is still religious. Is still Christian. I know that God is within us all, 'the light that lighteth every man that cometh into the world'.

Though poetry is not a religion, it is, like Jesus – like any rabbi – a teacher. It is heuristic. It will lead us to where the truth is. It will lead us to the heavenly host, whatever form that may take, and away from an obsession with the guinea. Poets know as well as St Paul that 'the love of money is the root of all evil'. That doesn't mean that the main topic of conversation when any poets meet isn't money. It is: but poets know that when they write with the guinea in mind, they don't write the truth.

The National Curriculum rightly tells us that good English teaching helps to promote spiritual education. To me there is an odd fit here, between curriculum's focus in this instance and its mechanistic structure. But we will take its advice, and I hope to suggest here some ways in which we can ensure that children look deeply into that part of themselves that is not tangible; that concerns (in Borges' phrase) 'the Holy Ghost, or the Muse, or the subconscious'; that focuses on my reiterated theme throughout this book, the heavenly Host rather than the guinea.

CHILDREN'S WRITING AND TRUTH

We will have to search somewhere in the children's poetry for truth. It won't be hard to find. Look, for example, at their writing in Chapter 2 based on the John Clare poem. Here they are antici- pating truths about what life will be like when they make dates with each other, assignations and trysts under the shade of oak trees or in the light of McDonald's restaurants. In the water poems in Chapter 3, they are under a human race-old fear of getting things wrong: they examine the water in the reproductions determined to tell the truth, of not letting any detail get away unnoticed and unrecorded. When they write about animals that have died, we can see their desperate reaching out for truth even, or perhaps especially, when they become sentimental. In their writing in imitation of Hardy's 'To the Moon', they address, however innocently, the biggest questions about the human race; questions that, like thousands of writers the world over, Hardy was addressing. The main one, in this poem, as in so many of his poems, is: 'Is it worth it?'

Adults behave as though they lose this need for the search for truth. The guinea, for all sorts of understandable reasons, takes over. The clouds of glory which we dragged, like the placenta, into the world thin out and disappear. We become desensitized to metaphysical truth, and obsessed with what we can know only with our senses. But the artist inside us, however free or imprisoned that artist may be, never loses sight of the heavenly host. The artist is walking through the world on a pilgrimage.

USING THE BIBLE

Creativity: 'That's Good!'

But, before truth, the first obvious link between poetry and religion is the word 'creativity'. The root of the word 'poet' is the Greek for 'maker', and in most religions, of course, God is the supreme Maker. In the assemblies that I lead in schools at the beginning of the day, I often tell children the Dylan Thomas anecdote I have quoted above, bowlderized, (inexcusably, but for forceful social reasons so I would plead) of the 'damn', and with Thomas' contemporary and unintentional (or innocent) sexism removed ('for the love of humankind'). I suggest to the children that, like God in the first thirty-four verses of Genesis, they should be able to look on whatever they might make today and say 'That's good.' Sometimes I read this passage to them:

> In the beginning God created the heaven and the earth. And the earth was without form, and void: and darkness was upon the face of the deep. And the spirit of God moved upon the face of the waters. And God said, Let there be light: and there was light. And God saw the light, that it was good; and God divided the light from the darkness. And God called the light Day, and the darkness he called Night. And the evening and the morning were the first day. And God said, Let there be a firmament in the midst of the waters, and let it divide the waters from the waters. And God made the firmament, and divided the waters which were under the firmament from the waters that were over the firmament; and it was so. And God called the firmament heaven. And

the evening and the morning were the second day. And God
said, Let the waters under the heaven be gathered together in
one place, and let the dry land appear: and it was so. And God
called the dry land Earth; and the gathering together called he
Seas: and God saw that it was good.

It was rewarding, comforting and educational to type those verses.
The rest can be found, of course, in any King James Version of the
Bible. Other versions are useful to make meanings clearer (*The New
Revised Standard Version*, *The Jerusalem Bible*, *The New English Bible*
and, if you are desperate for modern speech, *The New International
Bible* and *The Good News Bible*), but the King James has the confidence and the rhythms of faith. And it has magisterial Tudor
English, too. Sometimes I read to children James Weldon Johnson's
version of the creation. It begins 'And God stepped out on space /
And looked around and He said / 'I'm lonely. I'll make me a
world'. (This is from memory. I have lost my copy of the book in
which I found it.) Sometimes I read my version, 'At the very
beginning':

     At the very beginning
       the very beginning
   God made high up there
   and way down here
       at the very beginning
       the very beginning.

   And the earth was a shapeless nothing
   and darkness swam in the face
   of the deep, the terrible deep
       at the very beginning
       the very beginning.

   And God called on light
   and light came in like love,
   like love on a loveless land,
   and God saw the light was good
   and divisible into day
   and divisible into night
   and that was the first of days
       at the very beginning
       the very beginning.

And God called on an arch
in the middle of the waters
and he called the arch his heaven
and that was the second of days
    at the very beginning
    the very beginning.

And God called on the land
and the land came
and he called the land his earth
and the waters gathered together.
God called them the seas
and God saw that all was good
    at the very beginning
    the very beginning.

And God called on the grass
    herbs giving seed
        trees giving fruit
            flowers giving petals and perfume . . .
and God saw that all was good
and that was the third of days
    at the very beginning
    the very beginning.

And God called on the lights in his arch
to divide the day from the night
to tell how
    the seconds
     and minutes
      and hours
       and days
        and seasons
         and years
          and centuries
           and millennia
            travel and travel and travel
and travel . . .

and to give light to the earth.
There were two special great lights
to give light to the earth
and God saw that all was good
and that was the fourth of days

at the very beginning
the very beginning.

And from the waters came
creeping creeping animals
and birds flying in the arch
and whales turning in the waters
and God saw that all was good
and blessed them with new love
and told them to create
and that was the fifth of days
at the very beginning
the very beginning.

And then

aardvark and antelope
bee and bear and bass
and carp and carrion crow
and dogs and diana monkeys
and eland and elephant
at the very beginning
the very beginning
and fennec fox and finch
and Galapagos tortoises
and . . .
You can do the rest for yourselves.

And then God called on this
humankind which was
exactly like himself
exactly like himself
to rule over the alphabetic
bestiary (see above)
and blessed this humankind
male and female both
at the very beginning
the very beginning.

'Look what I've given you
and look after it all,

look after it all . . .'
and God saw that all was good,
not just good

                but very good,
not just very good, but

right, just, beautiful,
fit and proper, becoming,
lovely, wicked and smashing,
super and wonderful,
ace and hunky-dory . . .

and that was the sixth of days
   at the very beginning
   the very beginning.

And then God rested
and that was the seventh of days
   at the very beginning
   the very beginning
and he closed his bestiary
and all his wonderful books,
his massive dictionaries
and rested
            and rested
                    and rested

and rested

   at the very beginning
   the very beginning

I usually commandeer the children to use this poem in the same
way that the ancient Hebrews are believed to have used their
version of the creation. Thus, I divide the school into two parts,
with one part saying 'At the very beginning' and the other replying
'the *very* beginning', while I read the rest of the poem. If I have
enough time with the children, I get them to say, in groups, the
part I have usually allocated to myself.

   Long before I wrote this poem, and long before I understood the
power of writing as a learning tool (that is, part of a process rather
than simply a product) I asked a class of children to write their
own creation myths. A girl called Vashti wrote this story:

One day God said 'I'm lonely. I will make something to keep me
company.' He made a dog but the dog looked sad. 'What's the
matter?' Dog said, 'God I'm so lonely.'

So God made lots of dogs but they ate him out of house and home. So he said 'I will make you a world and you can live on it.' So he did. But there was not any light, or food, or water. So God got some fire and rolled it into a ball and threw it above the earth.

'I will call you Sun' said God, feeling really pleased.

But then something very strange happened. Bits of the sun kept falling off. It did not seem very pleased to be a ball in the sky. God grabbed what was left of the sun and took it apart. He put some clay in the middle of it and put it back in its place and the little bits of the sun that had fallen off the sun he called stars.

Then he sat on the edge of his garden with his legs dangling down into space. He stamped on his world and made holes in it. He went into a well and got water and put it into all the little holes.

Just then God's friend Mountain came along, stamping and shaking salt all over the place. 'Don't do that!' said God. 'Now look what you have done!' Mountain looked at God's world. There were lumps in it and the water was salt. God sat down and said 'Dear oh dear I wish there were not vibrations. I don't see why you had to stamp, Mountain. And as for shaking salt, look what you have done to my sea!'

But the dogs had guessed that this might happen, so they had made tunnels in the earth, and some of the fresh water had run into them. Then the dogs had found some un-dry clay and made a cover for them and called them river, steam, lake and spring.

Meanwhile God had decided to call all the lumps mountains after his friend. The dogs said 'We want food' so God made some other kinds of creatures and things for them to eat, but they argued about their food, so God made a chart for everyone, like this:

COW —— GRASS

Then the dogs went up to God. 'We want something to see and sleep on' they said.

So God made plants, shrubs, trees and grass. Then he went to bed.

The next day he got up. The dogs came round him and pestered him all morning for something to play with. In the end God got cross. 'Be satisfied' he said. So they went away from a very tired God.

He went straight to bed and the dogs made a plan. They got

all of God's clay and got in a long line. One by one they solemnly got some clay, threw it into the sky and named it.

There was Mars, Saturn and a lot of others. Then God woke up.

He decided to make the dogs something to do. He got his bag with clay in it. There was only a little bit. God knew at once it was the dogs, so he made them two things to make them work as a punishment. He called them humans. Then he ran out of clay.

Well, at least it gave the dogs something to do, and God was satisfied.

(Vashti, 9)

I have written earlier about teaching children to be critics by helping them to listen closely to literature, to perform it and to imitate it. Now let us try to be critics of this piece of writing.

First, Vashti begins with God's loneliness (implied in Genesis 1:26) then subverts the original by having God make (in a literal and playful reversal of his own name and image) a dog. Later she intensifies this subversion with her extraordinary ending: Man and Woman as companions for the senior animals, the dogs.

Second, she humanizes God: he thinks in terms of clichés that the writer might well have heard her parents use ('they ate him out of house and home'); he gets mildly grumpy – 'I don't see why you had to stamp, Mountain. And as for shaking salt, look what you have done to my sea!'. This is again, probably, like the writer's parents. His legs dangle down into space, like a child's when sitting on a wooden bridge catching crabs on bits of string baited with bacon. Vashti makes God fallible, which is certainly a problem for the theologically orthodox but which, it seems to me, is part of a child's coming to terms with her religion. How can you see God as infallible (assuming you eventually do) if you have never seen him as fallible?

Third, the rhythms of the piece are satisfying: the writer, whom I remember after thirty years as, amongst other things, a greedy reader of fiction, was influenced by the books she chose herself, the Bible story and by James Weldon Johnson's poem. This makes me reflect yet again how eager children are to learn; how, contrary to popular notion, hungry they are for new things. They are taking on new ideas, and new takes on old ideas, all the time. Fourth, the story has subtleties, like the mountain shaking the salt about, giving the sea part of its essence, and the dogs being responsible for the rivers.

I had learned nothing at the time I taught Vashti (1968) about teaching children to make drafts. Few teachers had. This piece is even more impressive given that it is a first draft: no chance for remaking, for draining redundant words, for expanding, for making more vivid. Thirty-two years later, in another school, a boy wrote his creation myth. I don't know what chance he had to redraft. I didn't teach him until after he had written his amazing story:

The Sun, the Moon, the World, the Beginning

In the beginning there was nothing but loneliness, emptiness, darkness. God was bored with this same old nothingness. He wanted a change of scenery. An idea sprang into his mind. A vision of what could emerge from this meaningless universe, of what it could be. God decided to make his dream a reality. First he made two different times. One where you could see and one where you couldn't. He would call one 'day' and one 'night'.

The next day God continued to create a different scene and feeling. Today he would make something, simple, something pure but at the same time incredibly necessary. He would call this 'water', and give it the property of being the backbone of life. With this he would make 'rivers', 'lakes', 'seas' and 'streams'. God still had time that day to make one more thing: a border between earth and heaven. He would call this sky. Heaven he had decided would be his home.

A new day, a new idea. God would make land in between the seas, and waters of rivers would scar the landscape. The land would also be covered in emerald green grasses. He would scatter the hills with brightly coloured flowers that would bear the colours of the rainbow that hung in the born sky.

A fifth day, today he would make the sky the home of a living creature. He would call it the bird and give it the gift of flight. He would make the sea the home of a creature he would call the fish. He would give it the ability to swim. He would make land the home of many creatures. He would call these beasts, each one with a different quality.

It was another day and God would get to work straightaway. Today he would make a fireball. He would call it the sun. It would give the earth he had made warmth and light. God would make what he called the moon. It would give a silvery light to the night. He scattered sequins all over the sky. They would shine out.

On the sixth day, God was quite happy, but not content. He still wanted a creature that was superior to all the rest. A creature with many-a-talent. He decided to make it out of clay. It would be in the same shape as himself. He would make one male (Adam) and one female (Eve). As I mentioned before water is the backbone of life so all it took to bring Adam and Eve to life was a drop of pure crystal clear water.

The final day of that week and the produce of six days' labour was displayed before God's eyes. For today God would rest and enjoy the company of humans, feeling proud of the universe sprung in completion, as well as the story I have just told.

(Prakash, 11)

This story is worth examination, as Vashti's is. A second reading (and children's writing is worthy of this compliment more often than many teachers think) will reveal, first, a stately, rhythmic prose. It is the prose of someone who enjoys his language. For example, 'loneliness, emptiness, darkness'; 'something, simple, something pure but at the same time incredibly necessary': the traditional triple of folk prose has seeped into Prakash's style. Everything happens in threes: in his world there has been three little pigs, three billy goats gruff and three bowls of porridge, and there will be one day, if he studies Shakespeare, three casks for the suitors to choose in *The Merchant of Venice*, three daughters for *Lear*, and three witches to counsel *Macbeth*. Prakash has internalized this principle, and shows the fruits of it in his myth.

Second, there is the surprising rightness of certain words: the rivers 'scar' the landscape. 'Hung in the born sky' is a perfect phrase. The beautifully placed archaism 'many-a-talent' suits this genre. But there is also the inappropriateness of 'backbone' for water: such an infelicity is something that we live with in clever writing by children. Other odd wrongnesses (the sun created after the animals and plants, for example) do not matter in the least, because that is part of the quality we notice, as modern humankind, as characteristic of myths – including the Biblical creation story. As Stephen Dedalus says in *Ulysses* (1922), 'The playwright who wrote the folio of this world . . . wrote it badly (He gave us light first and the sun two days later).' The occasional slight predictability in Prakash's writing does not matter either: the birds flying, the fish swimming. Prakash has hit on an essential truth: 'what could emerge from this meaningless universe'. Like a writer or a painter in their studio or study, looking at meaningless chaos, he wonders what shape can be made of it, with the help of water: 'all it took to bring Adam and Eve to life was a drop of pure crystal clear water'.

I note that the story refers to itself at the end. This cunning touch shows that Prakash is alive to all the fragments of prose around him – advertisements, CD liners, headlines – even though the phrase 'post-modernist' is almost certainly unknown to him.

Three things I understand not

Proverbs 30:18–9 have haunted me since I first heard them when I was a child:

> Three things are too wonderful for me; four I do not understand;
> the way of an eagle in the sky, the way of a snake on the rock;
> the way of a ship on the high seas; and the way of a man with a
> girl.

This is from the *New Revised Standard Version*: my preferred King James Version gives 'maid' for 'girl', but that word 'maid' has different connotations in the twenty-first century from those it had in the sixteenth. Children appreciate the rhythms of this piece of ancient Hebrew poetry in any version because the triplet, as I have said, runs all though our culture. Here, it is neatly subverted by the writer of Proverbs with a fourth component.

The little 'prison cell' of this was easily appreciated by one class, and the word 'wonderful' made things even easier for them:

> Three things are too wonderful for me
> no four
> my mum's kindness
> my cat's friendly purr
> my dad's soft voice
> and why there are cows.

(Samantha, 10)

> Three things are too wonderful for me
> no four I do not understand
> Whether people have second lives,
> why a special person in this class that I respect is funny,

why people with braces talk so odd
and why my dad sings for hours on end.

(Natasha, 11)

One, people with glasses that stare at men with horror.
Two, boys with very deep voices.
Three, teachers that are really nice.
Four, why are boys invented.

(Catherine, 10)

One, the way my cat hunts.
Two, the way my cat sleeps.
Three, the way my cat purrs.
And four, the way my cat laps up his milk.

(Freddie, 10)

I would have done better to read the whole of Proverbs 30 before
this lesson, because I would have come across other examples of
this structure. And they would have further enriched the lesson
and the work that the children did. Here is one example:

> There be four things which are little upon the earth, but they are
>   exceeding wise:
> the ants are a people not strong, yet they prepare their meat in the
>   summer;
> the conies are but a feeble folk, yet they make their house in the
>   rocks;
> the locusts have no king, yet go they forth all of them by bands;
> the spider taketh hold with her hands, and is in king's palaces.

(Proverbs 30:25–9)

Glory Be to God

While I am quoting the Old Testament, it is worth pointing out that
the last Psalm, 150, would work well alongside Gerard Manley
Hopkins' poem 'Pied Beauty' (in Gardner, 1948):

> Praise ye the Lord, praise God in his sanctuary: praise him in the
> firmament of his power. Praise him for his mighty acts: praise
> him according to his excellent greatness. Praise him with the
> sound of the trumpet: Praise him with the psaltery and the harp.
> Praise him with the timbrel and the dance: praise him with the

stringed instruments and organs. Praise him upon the loud cymbals: praise him upon the loud sounding cymbals. Let everything that hath breath praise the Lord. Praise ye the Lord.

Pied Beauty

Glory be to God for dappled things –
    For skies of couple-colour as a brinded cow;
    For rose-moles all in stipple upon trout that swim;
Fresh-firecoal chestnut falls; finches' wings;
    Landscape plotted and pieced – fold, fallow and plough;
      And all trades, their gear and tackle and trim.

All things counter, original, spare, strange;
    Whatever is fickle, freckled (who knows how?)
With swift, slow; sweet, sour; adazzle, dim;
He fathers-forth whose beauty is past change;
      Praise him.

In this next poem, it is clear that I have asked that the children should confine their references to a particular area of expertise. This girl celebrates her dog:

Glory be to God
for the lives of dogs
the barks and woofs
the scratchy sound when they're itchy,
the snarls, the yelps, grrrrr! yelp!
the nips and scratches when they play with you
the smell of dog fur, all damp and long.
their cold wet noses
and their long panting tongues
Glory be to God
for the sound of their claws touching
the ground as they walk up the garden path
the swish swash of their tails when they are happy
their snores when they are happily asleep
Glory be to God
for the horrible smell of dog food!

                          (Stephanie, 9)

AKHENATEN'S HYMN

I will not pretend that the writing that children have done in my company about religion has been in any way systematic. Nor has it been in the least representative of our society. I would like to have collected writing based on the other main religions, but I have not been able to do so. Most schools, however strongly other ethnic groups are represented, still embody a Christian hegemony. Other schools, I have found, respond to their multicultural pupil body by being safe: ignoring religious literature altogether, insofar as the National Curriculum allows them to do so.

This next beautiful glimpse into the nature of a dead religion comes through a hymn. It is reputed to have been written by the Pharaoh Akhenaten around 1500BC. Akhenaten was the 'heretic Pharaoh' who rejected the many gods of Egypt – Isis and Osiris and the rest – and insisted that the only god was the Aten, the sun disc. So many fascinating adjectives surround this strange man: monotheist, pacifist, misshapen, even hermaphrodite. Depending on who you read, he is a reformer, a 'disguised female', a eunuch, a mystic or the 'first individual in history'. Freud saw him as the forerunner of Moses, and others have seen him as a forerunner of Christ (Redford, 1987). Here is a version of part of his hymn:

You created the sun
when you were far away –
men, cattle, all flocks –
everything on the earth moving with legs,
creeping, stalking, striding,
flying or gliding above with wings.
Foreign countries and the land of Egypt:
you placed every man in his place
and you provide his food.

You are the Creator of months,
the Maker of days,
you are the counter of hours!

You shine on the eastern horizon
and fill the whole earth with your beauty
and while you are far away
your beams shine in every face.

When you shine
creatures live.
When you set
they die.
You yourself are lifetime.
In you do creatures live.

Living disc, Lord of all that was created
and which exists –
your beams have brightened
the whole earth.
    (Approx 1500BC. Version by Emily Roeves, in Sedgwick, 1997)

This famously resembles Psalm 104, which would also be appropriate to a lesson on this subject, and when I teach this lesson again, I will quote these verses from the Psalm:

Bless the Lord, O my soul. O Lord my God, thou art very great: thou art clothed with honour and majesty. Who coverest thyself with light as with a garment; who stretchest out the heavens like a curtain: who layeth the beams of his chambers in the water: who maketh the clouds his chariot: who walketh upon the wings of the wind . . .
    Who laid the foundations of the earth, that it should not be removed for ever . . .
    He watereth the hills from his chambers: the earth is satisfied with the fruit of thy works. He causeth the grass to grow for the cattle, and herbs for the service of man: that he may bring forth food out of the face of the earth . . . Thou makest darkness, and it is night: wherein all the beasts of the forest do creep forth . . .

I read the Akhenaten to a group of children many years ago, asking them to write their own hymn to the sun. I have kept this piece by me for over twenty years. It was written by the same girl who wrote the creation myth above:

You give your light up there in the sky,
golden sun,
like a big blob of paint:
yellow orange red and pink,
great big ball of fire.
You let the sky play with you –

the sky is your garden
and you are a prisoner in it.
You can never escape
however hard you try.
You are bleeding golden rays,
lighting up the world.
The world is your lightswitch.
Whenever it turns you shine.
Golden sun,
your rays wander down to the world
and play there,
great big monster
changing shape every minute.
You play hide and seek with the sky
hiding behind the clouds.
You are a dog.
The sky is your master.
Please make your rays
wander down to the earth today,
golden sun.

(Vashti, 8)

Note the evident enjoyment displayed in this writing. Connected with this, there is the tumbling confusion of the images. In twenty-six lines, the sun is a 'blob of paint', 'golden fire', a body 'bleeding golden rays', a child 'playing' and, finally, a dog. The sky is a 'garden', another child playing, and a dog's master. Of course, this material could have been better organized. It was written when I was in my first job and, much as I was putting my own early attempts at poems through numerous drafts, I did not know about the need for children to draft. Few teachers did.

I taught this lesson on Akhenaten fifteen years after the lesson in which Vashti's work appeared, and added to the mix both Vashti's work and Philip Larkin's poem 'Solar' (Larkin, 1977). This is also an address to the sun. One child wrote:

Your beams are water sprinklers spraying out.
You are a birthmark to the universe.
You are an eagle in the sky,
a flying electric blanket.
You are a pond of light.

The earth is just one of the planets full of fish
you have to care for.

(Anon., 10)

This work – not a poem, but certainly notes towards one – contains images that are almost ridiculously far-fetched. But I don't mind about that. I'd sooner the children's writing was strange rather than it was true, because aiming at strangeness helps the children to avoid cliché, which is the one sure killer of all writing; and truth will come, if the writer keeps on searching with pen and keyboard. It is better to take risks, to sound silly, than to use, in Barthes' phrase (1982) only 'the conforming, plagiarising edge' of language that gets us nowhere.

ABIKU, KAHINDE, TAIWO

This book is short on writing from ethnic minorities living in the United Kingdom. This is because I have deliberately concentrated on classical literature, and there is little literature from the classical periods available to us. Modern literature is, of course, rich in African and African-Caribbean writing: Langston Hughes, James Weldon Johnson, for example, and the moderns, Grace Nichols, John Agard, Benjamin Zephaniah, James Berry, David Dabydeen. A book like Grace Nichols' anthology *Poetry Jump-Up* (1993) demonstrates the riches available to teachers and readers, and Heaney and Hughes' *The Rattle Bag* introduced me in 1982 to the hunter poems of the Yoruba, translated by Ulli Beier.

I decided to focus on one cultural group about which I have some little knowledge through personal contact. I learned something about the religious beliefs of the Yoruba people of Nigeria when I did a BA degree with the Open University in the early 1970s. An enlightened Professor of Humanities, John Ferguson, felt that it was important that a foundation course in his subject should not be restricted to white western culture. This seems very outdated now, but at a time when a course of world religion could be called 'Man's [sic] Religious Quest', even a casual interest in an African culture in mainstream university courses was a radical diversion from the norm. So Ferguson's unit for the OU's Foundation Course, *The Yorubas of Nigeria* (1970), was a departure for its time. Ferguson wrote that 'to spend a week in examining societies with very different culture patterns [from our own] reminds us of the complex diversity of human experience ... and may enable us to understand ourselves better'. Much of my work below based on twins derives from this book.

Fifteen years later, my knowledge and understanding of the Yorubas was enhanced with a stroke of fortune. I was lucky enough to meet the Yoruba artist/poet Emmanuel Taiwo Jegede, who agreed to be an artist in residence at the primary school of which I was headteacher. He became for a time a friend, and illustrated pages in a poetry anthology on which I was working (Sedgwick, 1994). I also bought one of his pictures.

On the last day of his residency he recited one of his poems in Assembly, 'Ododo Ni Mi' – 'I was a flower'. The whole school from the youngest nursery child to the oldest Year 6 was there, in a celebratory mood: it was the end of a term. Emmanuel came to the front of the hall where I was standing in sunlight in front of the nursery children and said to me, 'You read it first in English.' The poem begins, in English:

I was a flower, a blossoming flower
Plucked from a bush by Olabisi . . .

When I'd finished reading the translation (by Gordon Tialobi) Emmanuel divided the school into two parts, and said to one half that they were to make a sound like 'oo-oo-oo' and to the other that they were to make a sound like 'ah-*ha*-sa'. Then, with both sides of his enormous human rhythm section going, he said his poem in its original Yoruba. There was a spontaneous round of applause, and afterwards the children were queuing up for Emmanuel's autograph.

I write this here as a glimpse of what Yoruba culture looks like to a modern primary school, and to show how a firsthand engagement with a culture different from our own is infinitely more effective than tokenistic work in multiculturalism: what has been dismissively called 'The Divali Curriculum'. It is through engagements like this that children may glimpse a paradox: we are very different from each other, but we are also the same. If we were dogs, we would all be the same breed, and a Yoruba farmer has more in common with a stockbroker in Kent than he has differences.

Encyclopaedia Britannica bears out a claim that Emmanuel Jegede made to me: Yorubas 'have traditionally been among the most skilled and productive craftsmen in Africa . . . In the 13th and 14th centuries Yoruba bronze casting . . . reached a peak of technical

excellence never subsequently equalled in west Africa'. Ferguson (1970) writes about 'the sheer quality of Yoruba culture in some fields . . . artistic expression in sculpture and dancing'. Jegede told me, 'The Yorubas are the artists, the money-makers, the politicians. They are the Jews of Nigeria.'

Yoruba religion involves a hierarchy of over four hundred gods, and the chief among them is Olorun. Many Yorubas combine their tribal religion with Islam or Christianity. Twins (like Emmanuel) are very common among the Yorubas, and are honoured. The first-born is seen as the younger, being sent out by his brother or sister to inspect the new country. He or she is called Taiwo. The second twin delays entry into the world, and is called Kahinde. The mother (who, with her family, celebrates such an auspicious event as the birth of twins) buys a pair of wooden figures called *ibeji*.

I possess a pair of *ibeji*, and I showed them to the children and told them about the *ibeji* cult. A weakling that dies early is called *abiku*. He or she is not a true child, but a fierce spirit returning to the wild. 'Such children', Ferguson tells us, 'are regarded with awe, and those who follow them are protected with charms'. I read to the children Wole Soyinka's poem that begins:

> In vain your bangles cast
> Charmed circles at my feet
> I am Abiku, calling for the first
> And the repeated time . . .
>
> I am the squirrel teeth, cracked
> The riddle of the palm . . .

(Soyinka, 1967)

The children wrote in the grip of this amazing poem:

Abiku

A wild place is where I belong.
All the blood and bones are mine forever.
Abiku I am.
The one who came out first.
I rule the world like a tiger that roars
But just better.

The blood and flesh is what I eat and drink.
I am best friends with the horrid spider.
That traps guilty flies
And what I like best
Is a shine like the brass pillar of the web.
Entering the world
I am abiku.
My twin is alive.
I'm not one of them.
My friends are where I am.
I am abiku.

(Matt, 10)

Abiku

Abiku is going to the wild.
Abiku is going to the world to live.
Abiku will live fearless forever in the wild
Never to be saved will Abiku
Living here in the black world of Abiku children.
Only to hear the laughs and cries and weird noises of the wild

the distant call of the howling wolf never to hurt a soul
living in nothingness but somewhere.
Abiku lives in the boggy, marshy, icy, stony, woody, dirty, dry,
    hot, damp, soft, sharp leaves of the wild . . .
Abiku is going to the wild.

(Anon., 9)

Taiwo is the first twin:

Taiwo

'Why me first oh brother?'
'I have to be cautious Little One.'
'But I don't know what it's like out there.'
'Neither do I, you must go, I am superior.'
'I shall be brave and go.'

What is this light
liquid all over me,
all these creatures?
What is this place
where I am going?
They wrap me up.
I hear crying.
My brother comes.
All is well.

'You made it Little One.'
'Yes I did.'
'I thank you Little One, you cleared the way.'
'I did it for you.
I hope you would do it for me
You are superior like me.'

(Thomas, 10)

Kahinde is the second twin who is deemed the older, having sent
his or her younger sibling out to see if the world is safe:

Kahinde

Get out there!
Check it out for me.
Don't come back
Till after tea.

This world's got to be perfect
For me.
I'll be the Sun's Prince
And the moon's light reflecting in the night.
Get off your bum
And get out there!
I am the world,
The only me.
Go on out, you've got a job to do.
There may be spiders, geckos, tigers too.
Be careful little brother
But clear the way for me.
Make some space
For little me.

                                                    (Jonathan, 10)

These poems show that the Soyinka poem and the Yoruba *ibeji* that I had showed the children had a powerful effect. Lines like 'All the blood and bones are mine forever', 'shine like the brass pillar of the web' and 'I'll be the Sun's Prince / And the moon's light reflecting in the night' are evidence of a culture working on these writers' minds and hearts. One can sense the process of learning in these lines, as indeed one could sense it in the atmosphere in the classroom – quiet, tense, and both emotional and intellectual. This process is even more important than the final poems, beautiful as they are, because the education is in that process.

One could go further. In his book, Stenhouse (1976) talks about three models for curriculum development: one that depends on identifying objectives and therefore striving towards them; one that emphasizes the process, therefore emphasizing the quality of the experiences that teachers are able to offer children; and finally, one that treats teachers as researchers of their own classrooms, a model that potentially sets children free to make their classrooms better places. I believe that it is wise to see these poems as examples of children engaging in mini research projects into themselves and into their relationship to a foreign culture.

At the same time as exploring a different culture through the medium of language, the children who wrote those lines were writing authentically from their English culture, robustly expressing both sibling aggression ('Get off your bum!') and, most movingly, at the end of Thomas' poem, brotherly affection.

As I write, I learn. This seems to be true of all writers who are not merely writing to entertain. Over the years I have collected different sentences in which this truth has been expressed. 'How can I tell what I think till I see what I say?' is variously attributed – to W. H. Auden, to E. M. Forster, and to an anonymous little girl quoted in Graham Wallas' *The Art of Thought* (found in Kemp, 1998). Doris Lessing said somewhere that 'You change as you write, you change yourself, you change the way you think.' And Geoffrey Grigson expresses the same kind of idea when he writes, 'How many of us in fact discover our convictions from what we write, instead of writing in obedience to known convictions?'

What am I conscious of learning during the course of writing this book? I wrote in Chapter 4 about my gradual and saddening discovery of moral relativity. I think now that to understand that morality is dependant on circumstances is not to be completely relativistic. Skelton writes (1978) that although poetry is 'constantly emphasising the subjectivity of the universe', the writing of poetry is not purely solipsistic. There is no 'completely anarchic view of morality' because 'poetry is, all the time, concerned to establish the wonderful complexity of human nature'. Quoting Pierre Emmanuel, Skelton insists that 'Poetry … teaches reverence for the individual.'

What a contrast this is to the ideas that have dominated the administration of education since 1980. This is that 'instrumental rationality' that signifies an obsession with 'How' rather than 'Why'. Gibson (1983) suggests that this represents the division of reason from feeling. I would say that this rational movement actually tries to make feelings irrelevant. It represents what Gibson calls 'the celebration of mastery', which will always be the celebration of the guinea as well.

This is the one holy truth: John Keats knew it, or even discovered it, as he wrote to Benjamin Bailey: 'I am certain of nothing but the holiness of the heart's affections and the truth of the imagination.' For poetry, in Emmanuel's definition, read all the kinds of writing in this book that are written in the integrity of the search for truth, with the imagination stretched to its extremes, and the holiness of the heart's affections unquestioned. This reverence is where the relativism breaks down and where, as writers, all human beings are on firm ground. It is where 'the Holy Ghost, or the Muse, or the subconscious' are witness.

Appendices

1   A NOTE ABOUT INFORMATION AND COMMUNICATIONS TECHNOLOGY

I have written something like the following words before (Sedgwick, 2000e), but I find that now I need them again:

Despite the computer developments that have taken place over the past twenty-odd years, inside and outside schools, children do very little word processing in classrooms. The computer's strengths in this area are largely restricted to labels for display and for what are called 'fair copies'. This sells computers and, rather more importantly, children short. It neglects a massive contribution that ICT (Information Communication Technology) can make to our teaching of English.

First, computers take away much clerical drudge from writing. As I write this, I recall how, when using a manual typewriter in the 1970s, I had to tippex mistakes out and then fiddle about with the carbon, making the ends of my fingers blue, as though the work had given me a form of frostbite. Once the number of mistakes had risen to three or four or so, you had to swear, shrug and retype. Adding paragraphs to an apparently finished page meant using a new sheet, with asterisks and arrows all over it to show where it had to go, and then, of course, retyping the whole lot in its new form. All this was true – even more so – for hand-written scripts.

Second, computers (and this is far more important) change our way of thinking about what we are writing about. This latter point arises from the fact that using a word processor, I can change the order of these paragraphs within a minute by using cut and paste; on Windows, Control C and Control V. I highlight a passage, press Control C, and the passage is held; I move the cursor, press Control V and that passage is now in its new position. If I press Delete after holding the passage in Control C, it will be in its new position. If I don't, I will have the passage now in two positions. I have found that this practice has actually made my way of thinking more flexible. Walking along a street, I can reorder my thoughts for a lecture or an article with this word processing model in mind. Children need opportunities to work with first drafts on computers so they can get the benefit that those computers bring of liberating their thinking.

A third use of computers is that they help children to publish their work in the classroom and the school, in order to make it more readable. This means that children can make documents that are readable, in the limited, literal sense, for each other to read.

I would add here a further point. Schools that can afford to do so have often developed what is proudly termed their 'computer suite': a range of gleaming machines round the walls of a carpeted room, arranged like cookers in a home economics laboratory. Casual observation in many schools over the past two years has suggested to me that the purpose of this suite is more to impress visitors than to help children to learn. Indeed, often, it is empty of children. When it is full, it is often full of children with a teacher 'doing ICT', or playing games during a wet lunch hour. But this raises an interesting question. Is ICT a subject at all? While I accept that children need to become efficient with computers, I would insist that computing is not a subject, as are English or History or Geography, but a tool for all subjects.

The best state of affairs for English is to have two or three computers in every classroom, each equipped with a printer. The most successful ICT that I have seen was in Warwick Road Special School in Bishop Auckland. In this school, every writer in my groups of fourteen or so children had a computer on which to work – a desk computer or a laptop. This school seemed better equipped than most to be able to meet the requirements of the TTA's ICT documents for schools.

2　A SUGGESTED LESSON PLAN

A lesson plan would look something like this:

My Aims for This Lesson

Children will use words by [take any writer represented in this book, or some other writer] to learn about two things.

First, this learning is about themselves. All personal, creative writing involves a process of self-discovery, and this is the most important aspect of it.

Second, the children will learn about the literature passage. They will do this by composing the first draft of a new piece of writing: this writing is a way of responding actively rather than passively to the work chosen for the lesson.

I aim that the children will enjoy the words, so there will be no element of anything that might resemble 'drill'. In contrast, children will play with the passage: by reciting it after me, by filling in missing words, by saying parts of it themselves. They might have a copy of the passage in front of them, but this is not necessary.

Introduction: Familiarize the children with the chosen passage in as many ways as possible (see paragraph above).

Suggest ways in which the children might use the words to begin their own writing.

Give the children a minute or two of intense silence in which they think about this, composing phrases in their heads. When their hands shoot up because they have thought of a phrase, increase the burden: you want two phrases; three; four. Children with their hands up are not learning, merely competing. The more silence you can help the children find, the greater the quality of what they will think of and, later, produce.

The class listens to some of the phrases, and comments on each others' ideas.

The children will write. I tell the children that the classroom, or library, or school, or wherever we are working, has now become a study, and therefore no sounds are allowed. This writing will be interrupted by plenary sessions every twenty minutes or so when the children share what they have written, and help each other to edit drafts. During the final plenary, children will read, in as polished a way as possible, their drafts. This session will be an evaluation, as well, as everybody can begin to judge the quality of the teaching, the learning and the poems written.

3 'THE CHILDREN ROUND HERE'

I wonder how many times I have been told in a staffroom that 'The children round here aren't very creative', or 'You won't get much out of the children round here because of their backgrounds'. They 'don't have much language at home'; 'We have to begin with the absolute basics when they come to us.' One special needs teacher told me that one child 'hadn't started', while Hughes (1989) quotes another teacher saying that her children come 'with nil on entry'. The kinds of schools where teachers say these things, and other things related to them, are surprisingly varied. Of course, it is said in schools that serve entirely working-class children, but I have also had it said to me in schools in middle-class areas. When I was a young teacher, first in Stevenage and then in Berkhamsted, I said things like this myself.

In the 1980s I read two books that changed my mind about this: Tizard and Hughes (1984) and Wells (1986). Put crudely, these writers' researches into homes and schools suggest strongly that the school's curriculum is narrower than the home's, and that passages of intellectual search by children are largely absent at nursery schools and are happening almost all the time in all sorts of homes. All three writers dispute (and, in my opinion, refute) the notion that working-class homes are, linguistically, deserts. The ones that Tizard and Hughes saw were 'a rich source of learning opportunities . . . most children start school with considerable intellectual capacities'. Wells says that 'children are restricted by the style of pupil–teacher interaction that [is] so typical of classrooms'. Children, when they come into school, are forced to become accustomed to a discourse that is entirely alien to them: administrative, managerial, clerical, even interrogatory. The kind of discourse that they are used to – based on genuine enquiry and need for information ('Would you like some more potatoes?' 'Would you like to go to the park or the swimming pool?') – is absent. Is it then surprising that they respond to the school discourse in terms of their home discourse and, in the teachers' eyes, get it wrong? Children come to school with a thousand different things to say, but we restrict them to responses to questions like 'Will you open that window for me, please?' or 'Would you do that at home?' or 'Was that a very nice thing to say, Justin?'. By restricting children to school-type discourse, we ignore their knowledge of non-school subjects: fishing, dancing, football, cycling, even travel. We ignore the fact that, in terms of the discourse that they use at home, they are already language experts.

The most telling passage in these books is in Wells: 'Rosie: a learning-disabled child?'. I have not the space or time here to develop or even describe very fully this argument. All I will say is that by assuming the best of children and their backgrounds – for example, by assuming that homes are rich places rather than deserts – we will get more from them in school. If we show genuine interest in what children say, they will be exposed as the efficient users of language that nearly all of them are. If, on the other hand, we accept the almost universally accepted (among teachers at any rate) desert argument, and restrict our talks with children to school discourse, both our manner of speaking to them and the content of what we say will encourage them to fail. And that will encourage the system to label them 'failures'.

The passages from literature that I have quoted in this book will appeal – some more than others – to all children between the ages of 8 and 13 if we read the passages with spirit, and if we respect the children to the extent of expecting them to enjoy what we read, and write imaginatively in the grip of it. The 'children round here' are as creative as we in schools allow them to be.

References and bibliography

The multitude of books is a great evil. There is no measure
or limit to this fever of writing; everyone must be an author;
some out of vanity to acquire celebrity; others for the sake
of lucre or gain. (Martin Luther, 1569)

Abse, Dannie (1970) *Selected Poems.* London: Hutchinson.

Adcock, Fleur (2000) *Poems 1960–2000.* Newcastle: Bloodaxe.

Albee, Edward (1962) *Who's Afraid of Virginia Woolf.* London:
Penguin.

Aubrey, John [1690] 'Brief Lives'. First published in Anthony Wood,
Athenae Oxoniensis.

Auden, W. H. (1971) *A Certain World: A Commonplace Book.* London:
Faber.

Auden, W. H. (1976) *Collected Poems.* London: Faber.

Auden, W. H. (1977) *The English Auden: Poems, Essays and Dramatic
Writings 1927–1939,* (ed.) Edward Mendelson. London: Faber.

Bagnall, Nicholas (1973) *New Movements in the Study and Teaching of
English.* London: Temple Smith.

Bain, E., Morris, J. and Smith, R. (1996) (eds) *King Lear.* Cambridge:
Cambridge University Press.

Barfield, Owen (1953) *History in English Words.* London: Faber.

Barthes, Roland (1982) *A Barthes Reader,* ed. by and with an introduction by Susan Sontag. London: Jonathan Cape.

Benét, William Rose (1973) *The Reader's Encyclopaedia.* London: Book
Club Associates.

Berry, M. and Clamp, M. (1994) (eds) *Antony and Cleopatra.* Cambridge: Cambridge University Press.

Birkett, Julian (1983) 'Embroidery' by Emily Bishop from Working
Lives in *Word Power: A Guide to Creative Writing.* London: A. &
C. Black.

Blake, William (1810) 'A Vision of the Last Judgement', descriptive catalogue. Quoted in *The Oxford Dictionary of Quotations*, 3rd edn. Oxford: Oxford University Press.

Bloom, Harold (1994) *The Western Canon: The Books and School of the Ages*. London: Macmillan.

Boswell, James [1791] (1906) *The Life of Samuel Johnson LL.D.* London: Dent.

Browne, Ann (1993) *Helping Children to Write*. London: Paul Chapman.

Buckle, L. and Kelly, P. (1992) (eds) *A Midsummer Night's Dream*. Cambridge: Cambridge University Press.

Burgess, Anthony (1964) *Nothing Like the Sun: A Story of Shakespeare's Love Life*. London: Vintage.

Carpenter, Humphrey (1992) *Benjamin Britten: A Biography*. London: Faber and Faber.

Carroll, Lewis [1865] (1978) *Alice's Adventures in Wonderland*. London: Jupiter Books.

Carroll, Lewis [1871] (1978) *Alice Through the Looking Glass and What Alice Found There*. London: Jupiter Books.

Carter, Ronald and McRae, John (1997) *The Routledge History of Literature in English: Britain and Ireland*. London: Routledge.

Clare, John (1996) *Selected Poems*. (ed.) Ian Hamilton. London: Bloomsbury.

Clegg, Alec (1965) *The Excitement of Writing*. London: Chatto and Windus.

Cotton, John (2000) *Poems From and About the Past*. London: Longman.

Cotton, John and Sedgwick, Fred (1996) *Two by Two*. Ipswich: Tricky Sam!

Cotton, John and Sedgwick, Fred (2000) *The Ammonite's Revenge*. Ipswich: Tricky Sam!

Crossley-Holland, Kevin (1968) *The Oxford Book of Travel Verse*. Oxford: Oxford University Press.

Crossley-Holland, Kevin (1979) *The Exeter Book of Riddles*. London: Penguin.

Crossley-Holland, Kevin and Sail, Laurence (1999) *The New Exeter Book of Riddles*. London: Enitharmon.

Dickens, Charles [1843] (1992) *A Christmas Carol*. London: W. H. Smith.

Dickens, Charles [1849–50] (1996) *David Copperfield*. London: Penguin.

Dunn, Douglas (1985) *Elegies*. London: Faber.

216   *References and Bibliography*

Ferguson, John (1970) *The Yorubas of Nigeria*. Bletchley: Open University.

Fowler, H. W. (1965) *A Dictionary of Modern English Usage*, 2nd edn. Oxford: Oxford University Press.

Gardner, W. H. (1948) (ed.) *Poems of Gerard Manley Hopkins*. Oxford: Oxford University Press.

Gibson, Rex (ed.) (1983) *The Education of Feeling*. Cambridge: Institute of Education.

Gibson, R. (1992) (ed.) *Romeo and Juliet*. Cambridge: Cambridge University Press.

Gibson, R. (1993) (ed.) *Macbeth*. Cambridge: Cambridge University Press.

Gibson, R. (1995) (ed.) *The Tempest*. Cambridge: Cambridge University Press.

Gray, M. (1984) *A Dictionary of Literary Terms*. Harlow: Longmans.

Gill, R. (1977) (ed.) *As You Like It*. Oxford: Oxford University Press.

Hamilton, Ian (1994) *The Oxford Companion to Twentieth-Century Poetry in English*. Oxford: Oxford University Press.

Hardy, Thomas (1976) *Collected Poems*, (ed.) J. Gibson. London: Macmillan.

Harrison, Michael and Stuart-Clark, Christopher (1977) *The New Dragon Book of Verse*. Oxford: Oxford University Press.

Hawkins, John (1787) in Kemp (1998).

Heaney, Seamus and Hughes, Ted (1982) *The Rattle Bag*. London: Faber.

Hill, Wayne F. and Ottchen, Cynthia J. (1994) *Shakespeare's Insults: Educating Your Wit*. Cambridge: MainSail Press.

Hogg, James (1824) *The Private Memoirs and Confessions of a Justified Sinner*.

Holbrook, David (1961) *English for Maturity*. Cambridge: Cambridge University Press.

Hughes, Martin (1989) 'The Child as Learner: the Contrasting Views of Developmental Psychology and Early Education', in Desforges, C. (ed.), *Early Childhood Education, British Journal of Educational Psychology* Monograph 4. Scottish Academic Press.

Hughes, Ted (1967) *Poetry in the Making*. London: Faber.

Jacobs, Alan (1997) *The Element Book of Mystical Verse*. Shaftesbury: Element.

Joyce, James [1992] (1993) *Ulysses*. Oxford: Oxford University Press.

Keats, John [1819] in Keegan (2000).

Keegan, Paul (ed.) (2000) *The New Penguin Book of English Verse*. London: Penguin.

Keillor, Garrison (1986) *Lake Wobegon Days.* London: Faber and Faber.

Kemp, Peter (1998) *The Oxford Dictionary of Literary Quotations.* Oxford: Oxford University Press.

Kipling, Rudyard (1928) in Kemp (1998).

Koestler, Arthur (1976) 'The Vision that Links the Poet, the Painter and the Scientist'. Opening address to the Conference of the PEN worldwide association of writers, Queen Elizabeth Hall, London, 24 August 1976. Reprinted in *The Times*, 25 August 1976.

Larkin, Philip (1964) *The Whitsun Weddings.* London: Faber.

Larkin, Philip (1970) *All What Jazz: A Record Diary 1961–1968.* London: Faber and Faber.

Larkin, Philip (1973) *The Oxford Book of Twentieth Century Verse.* Oxford: Oxford University Press.

Larkin, Philip (1977) *High Windows.* London: Faber.

Larkin, Philip (1988) *Collected Poems,* (ed.) Anthony Thwaite. London: Faber.

Le Faye, Deirdre (1995) (ed.) *Jane Austen's Letters.* Oxford: Oxford University Press.

Levin, Jonathan (1997) (ed.) *Poetry for Young People.* New York: Sterling Publishing.

Luther, Martin [1569] 'Table-Talk' in Kemp (1998).

Mackay, David (1969) *A Flock of Words: An Anthology of Poetry for Children and Others.* London: The Bodley Head.

Massingham, Hugh and Massingham, Pauline (undated) *The London Anthology.* London: Spring Books.

Mole, John (1987) *Once There Were Dragons.* London: André Deutsch.

Montague, John (1874) (ed.) *The Faber Book of Irish Verse.* London: Faber.

Murray, Les (1991a) *Collected Poems.* Manchester: Carcanet.

Murray, Les (1991b) *Dog Fox Field.* Manchester: Carcanet.

Nichols, Grace (1993) *Poetry Jump-Up.* London: Puffin.

Nye, Robert (1977) *Falstaff.* London: Hamish Hamilton.

Oliver, H. J. (1956) (ed.) *Timon of Athens.* London: Routledge.

Opie, Iona and Opie, Peter (1973) *The Oxford Book of Children's Verse.* Oxford: Oxford University Press.

Panichas, George A. (1977) *The Simone Weil Reader.* New York: David McKay.

Pollard, Andrew and Tann, Sarah (1987) *Reflective Teaching in the Primary School.* London: Cassell.

Pope, Alexander (1956) *Collected Poems.* London: Dent.

Redford, Donald B. *Akhenaten: The Heretic King.* Princeton, New Jersey: Princeton University Press.

Robson, J. (1973) (ed.) 'Borges on Poetry' in *Poetry Introduction 1.* London: Abacus.

Roeves, Emily. Various personal communications and unpublished sources.

Rosen, Michael (1982) *I See a Voice.* London: Hutchinson.

Rosen, Michael (1994) *The Penguin Book of Childhood.* London: Viking.

Rossetti, Christina (1911) *The Poetical Works*, with memoir and notes by William Michael Rossetti. London: Macmillan.

Sampson, George (1975) *English for the English.* Cambridge: Cambridge University Press.

Santini, L. (1991) *Pompeii, Vesuvius, Herculaneum.* Rome: Plurigraf.

Searle, Chris (1983) *Wheel Around the World.* London: Macdonald.

Sedgwick, Fred (1986) *The Living Daylights.* Liverpool: Headland.

Sedgwick, Fred (1988) 'The Sifter's Story: Experiences of a Poetry Competition' in *Cambridge Journal of Education* Vol. 18 No. 1.

Sedgwick, Fred (1994) 'Twenty Children' and 'Advice' in *Collins Primary Poetry.* London: HarperCollins.

Sedgwick, Fred (1997) *Read My Mind: Young Children, Poetry and Learning.* London: Routledge.

Sedgwick, Fred (1999a) *Thinking About Literacy: Young Children and their Language.* London: Routledge.

Sedgwick, Fred (1999b) *Shakespeare and the Young Writer.* London: Routledge.

Sedgwick, Fred (2000a) *Jenny Kissed Me: Poems about Love.* Birmingham: Questions.

Sedgwick, Fred (2000b) *Forms of Poetry 1.* Dunstable: Belair.

Sedgwick, Fred (2000c) *Forms of Poetry 2.* Dunstable: Belair.

Sedgwick, Fred (2000d) *Themes for Poetry.* Dunstable: Belair.

Sedgwick, Fred (2000e) *Writing to Learn: Literacy and Poetry across the Primary Curriculum.* London: Routledge.

Sellers, Susan (ed.) (1991) *Taking Reality by Surprise: Writing for Pleasure and Publication.* London: The Women's Press.

Skelton, Robin (1978) *Poetic Truth.* London: Heinemann.

Soyinka, Wole (1967) *Idanre.* London: Methuen.

Steiner, George (1989) *Real Presences.* London: Faber.

Stenhouse, Laurence (1976) *An Introduction to Curriculum Design and Development.* London: Heinemann.

Stevenson, Robert Louis [1886] (1991) *Kidnapped.* London: Reader's Digest.

Strachey, Lytton (1928) *Elizabeth and Essex: a Tragic History.* London: Chatto and Windus.

Thomas, Dylan (1952) *Collected Poems.* London: Dent.

Thomas, Edward (1978) *The Collected Poems of Edward Thomas,* (ed.) George R. Thomas. Oxford: Oxford University Press.

Tizard, Barbara and Hughes, Martin (1984) *Young Children Learning: Talking and Thinking at Home and at School.* London: HarperCollins.

Trollope, Anthony (1857) *Barchester Towers* (Everyman edition). London: Dent.

Weil, H. and Weil, J. (1997) *Henry IV, Part 1.* Cambridge: Cambridge University Press.

Wells, Gordon (1986) *The Meaning Makers: Children Learning Language and Using Language to Learn.* London: Hodder and Stoughton.

Wilde, Oscar (1990) *The Importance of Being Earnest* and *Lady Windermere's Fan.* Leicester: Bookmart.

Wilson, Anthony and Hughes, Sian (1998) *The Poetry Book for Primary Schools.* London: The Poetry Society.

Wright, William (1987) [1895] *An Account of Palmyra and Zenobia with Travels and Adventures in Bashan and the Desert.* London: Darf Publishing.

Compact Disc

'Songs and Dances from Shakespeare'. (1995) The Broadside Band, director Jeremy Barlow. Oxford: Past Times.

Index

Meeting the Requirements

A list of issues raised in DfEE, TTA and QCA documents (listed on page 4) implicitly and explicitly addressed in this book; also references to the National Literacy Strategy.